STRESS SIZE

Copyright © 2020 Nicole Starbuck

All rights reserved. No part of this book may be reproduced or used in any manner without written permission of the publisher except for the use of quotations in a book review.

ISBN: 978-1-7346432-0-6 (paperback)
ISBN: 978-1-7346432-1-3 (eBook)

Cover, Interior Design, and Typesetting by Dania Zafar
Editing by Robin J. Samuels
Proofreading by Lynda Dietz

Published by Nicole Starbuck
www.nicolestarbuck.com

STRESS SIZE

How My Hunger for Control Almost Killed Me

NICOLE STARBUCK

*To my husband, Raleigh (aka, Babycorn).
Thank you for saving me.*

Prologue

A DOUBLE VIOLIN CONCERTO WAS THE SOUNDTRACK TO MY death. Second movement, F major. How ironic that my life should end to the harmonious swells of my husband's favorite piece of music. Simply beautiful. Tragic, really. The genius, however, was difficult to appreciate amidst the present circumstances. I was suffocating.

My violent cries, not the least bit dampened by the pillow against my lips, drowned out the music Raleigh had put on in an effort to calm me. But I could not be consoled. How could I be, when my arms and legs were numb and my body was writhing uncontrollably? As I attempted to suck down air, I choked on the pillowcase now sopping with tears.

So this was how it was going to be—death by pillowcase to the tune of classical music. Perhaps it was better that way. No doctors, no hospital bills, no fuss. Minus the spasms and my incessant screaming, I could drift away peacefully. My life would be short, but at least I would be free from the stress. No more frantic schedules, no more corporate grind. I would finally be at peace.

Cry after cry, I waited. But death wouldn't come—only more and more sobs. I buried my face deeper into the pillow and prayed for the end of my existence, or at least a coma to render me unconscious. Anything to make the pain go away.

"Nicole?" my husband asked as he walked back into the room.

A serenade for strings in E major swooned in the background. "Nicole, can you hear me?"

I could, but he seemed so far away. My lips refused to budge. My eyes shut themselves tighter and I cried even louder.

"If you can hear me, I need you to tell me what's wrong."

He waited there, one hand on my shoulder, the other pulling the pillow away from my face so I could breathe. Didn't he know that I wanted the pillow in my face—that I wanted to die?

"Nicole," he stated firmly, but I still couldn't answer. There was a wall of tears between us. I couldn't break through. "Nicole, if you haven't calmed down in an hour, I'm taking you to the hospital," he warned. He left me to resume my self-inflicted suffocation.

And there it was—the threat, the prospect of a two- or three-thousand-dollar bill looming over me if I went to the hospital to figure out what was happening to me. Faced with such an immense burden, it was so much simpler to die, to let the tear-soaked pillowcase take my breath away.

Please kill me.

My body, with my legs tangled in the bedsheet and my arms pressed tightly against my chest, fell into a haphazard rhythm of sob, suck, shout, spasm, sob, suck, shout, spasm. Any moment would be the last. After all, the only sensation I could still feel was the immense pressure in my chest and the weight of two thousand dollars on my shoulders.

Sob, suck, shout, spasm. Why was this taking so long?

Let me die.

With the final flute flourish of an orchestral suite, my husband burst into the room. "Okay, that's it," he announced. "I'm taking you to the hospital."

"No!" I finally cried. "No! No! No! No!" But he wouldn't hear it. He lifted me into his arms and carried me downstairs to the car.

STRESS SIZE

The cold air bit through my body to my bones. I kept screaming for him to stop, to leave me alone, to let me die. But he wouldn't listen. Somehow, he managed to position my wildly kicking body into the backseat of the car.

So I was wrong. *This* was how my life was going to end—tears spewing, lungs collapsing, and my husband swerving through an unfamiliar part of town. Eyes glued shut. Arms tingling. Legs kicking crazily against the back of the passenger seat. With my body writhing and my mind slipping away, there could be no other explanation. I was going to die.

We came to an abrupt stop. The car doors opened and voices drifted in and out. "What's wrong?" somebody asked.

"I don't know," my husband replied frantically. "She's been like this for hours."

Hands reached into the car and grabbed me, shook me, and thumped my chest with a thud that resonated through my bones. My eyes fluttered open briefly, revealing a glimpse of a stranger, and then re-shut. The hands pulled me out of the car and plopped my limp body into a wheelchair. My legs crashed against the metal, and suddenly I was in motion. The winter air pierced my skin as the stranger wheeled me into the warmth of the waiting room.

"What's going on?" another voice asked.

"I don't know," my husband cried. "I don't know."

An attendant pulled down my shirt and pressed stickers all over my chest. "Vitals are fine," she replied.

Someone was screaming in the background.

A man yelled back, "Ma'am, you need to calm down!"

The screaming continued.

"Ma'am, I need you to calm down! There are other people here."

The screaming wouldn't stop.

"Ma'am, I need you to stay still," the man stated. "I can't help you if you keep moving."

My legs kept kicking.

"She won't stay still," the man complained. "I can't get the needle in."

"What's wrong with her?" someone asked.

"I don't know," Raleigh said. "She was in the bathroom getting ready for work, and suddenly she was on the floor."

The screaming grew louder.

"Get her into a room," someone ordered.

"We don't have any rooms," someone else said.

"Get her into a room," the voice repeated.

I realized I was the one screaming. I continued screaming until I ran out of air and finally passed out.

◆

"Nicole, can you hear me?" someone asked from miles away.

Yes, I can hear you.

"Can you hear me?" he repeated, closer.

My eyes cracked open a small, dim sliver. A stranger stood before me, awaiting my reply. Hadn't I already answered? My tongue was stuck.

"Do you know what happened?" he asked my husband.

"I don't know," he replied. "She was in the bathroom, and all of a sudden she was on the floor."

"Did she crash to the floor or kind of sink down?" he asked.

"I don't know," my husband admitted. "By the time I found her, she was crying and shaking uncontrollably. She said she couldn't breathe."

"I see," the doctor stated. He turned toward me. "Nicole, if you can hear me, I need you to nod your head."

My chin mustered a tilt.

"Okay." He nodded back. "I'm the emergency room doctor. I need to talk to you about what happened, okay?"

Another tilt.

"Are you on any medications?" he asked.

Left, right, slowly.

"Have you taken any drugs?"

Left, right, again.

"Can you tell me what happened?"

Can I? I wondered.

He waited.

"I was getting ready for work," I whispered. "I was brushing my teeth."

"Okay, good," the doctor replied. "What happened next?"

"I was brushing my teeth, and suddenly I felt very sick. Tired, and heavy, like I needed to sleep."

The doctor nodded.

"But I had to be at work. I couldn't call out. I had to be at work."

"What do you do?"

"I'm an assistant store manager."

"Do you work a lot?"

"Too much. I feel like I never have any time."

"Okay, so when you were brushing your teeth and you felt sick, what did you do?"

"I laid down on the floor. I wanted to sleep. But I had to be at work. I didn't have a choice. What were they going to do without me? I had to be there—I'm the closing store manager."

"That sounds like a lot of pressure," the doctor said.

"It's too much stress," I cried. "It's too much stress and I hate it."

"So you were thinking about work, and all the stuff you had to do, and what happened?"

"I started crying," I answered. "I started crying and I couldn't stop. I felt like I couldn't breathe, and then my arms and legs went numb. Raleigh came in and I asked him to call my boss to tell her that I couldn't come in."

"And then what?"

"I don't know," I replied.

"I carried her to the bedroom," Raleigh interjected. "I tried to put on some calming music. I thought maybe she just needed to rest."

"Did that help?" the doctor asked.

"I don't think so," he replied. "She kept crying. She cried for almost an hour. I thought she was dying—she wasn't breathing right and she wasn't responding."

"Well, you did the right thing by bringing her in," he said, glancing at my frail frame tucked beneath the thin sheet. "She's going to be okay. I have a few more questions and we'll get this all figured out." Raleigh nodded and squeezed my hand. Had he been holding it the whole time? The doctor turned his attention back to me. "So, Nicole, at any point during all of this, did you have any thoughts about killing yourself?"

My tongue was stuck again.

He waited.

"I wanted to die," I admitted. "I didn't want to be here anymore."

"Did you make any plans at all?" he asked. "Did you think about how you would do it?"

Raleigh looked concerned. I shifted uncomfortably. "Bleach, or something," I said. "Pills, maybe. I don't know. I'm not really sure."

"I see," the doctor replied. "Had you ever had any of these thoughts before?"

All the time, I thought. "I have a history of depression," I admitted.

"Hmm," the doctor murmured. Judgment washed over me. I waited for his response. "Based on what you've told me, it appears that you've had an anxiety attack," he concluded.

"I don't understand. An anxiety attack about what?"

"Work, stress, life in general," he replied. "Sometimes it builds up and gets triggered by any little thing."

"But that doesn't make any sense," I contested. "I'm not anxious."

"Maybe you don't think you are, but you are."

"But I'm not," I argued. "I want to go home."

"Okay, that's fine, but I can't let you go unless I know that you're not going to do anything to hurt yourself. I have to be confident you'll be safe. Are you going to hurt yourself?"

"No," I replied. That was probably a lie, but I didn't care. I wanted to leave.

"As long as you can assure me you're going to keep yourself safe, you can go home. But I want you to follow up with a psychiatrist, get this checked out, okay?"

"I'll think about it."

"Yes, please do. It's important. I'm going to send a nurse in to talk to you about some prescription medication for anxiety, okay?"

"I don't want any medication."

"Why not?"

"I just don't."

"Well, think about it."

"I'll think about it," I lied.

"Okay." He nodded at me, briefly met Raleigh's concerned gaze, and slipped around the curtain, leaving it closed.

Raleigh rubbed my ice-cold hand. "Do you want to talk about it?"

"No." I didn't want to talk about it. I wanted to write about it. I wanted to tell the world how I ended up in such a dark, desperate place, and how at the bottom of the pit of despair, the Universe revealed that it wasn't time for me to die.

   It was time for me to quit.

Chapter 1

THE WARNING SIGNS HAD MANIFESTED THEMSELVES LONG before my symbolic death. Hints appeared while we were still living in the desert, but in my incessant quest for control I ignored them. I had a plan, and all the details had to be just right. I couldn't wait around for my life to happen. I couldn't wait around for the Universe to make things happen. It was taking too long. I needed to take matters into my own hands.

"You should get it!" my husband yelled from across the living room as I plotted my course of action. Because of the sweltering heat, he was sitting on the sofa in nothing but boxers. The thick blackout curtains, even stretched out their entire width, scarcely covered the oversized window behind him. Slivers of sun slipped through the cracks on either side, heating the already warm room rather intensely. Sweating profusely was an everyday reality in the summer, especially in this house.

The swamp cooler roared in my ear. "What?" I shouted back. Also wearing nothing but my underwear, I sat uncomfortably on the wicker chair in front of the elongated side table I had commandeered as my work station. Even sitting still made me sweat in that sauna of a living room. I was fortunate that my long list of tasks could be completed on the laptop set up in front of me. My arms and hands were numb from pressing my elbows onto the desk as I stared at the computer screen contemplating the purchase, but at least I didn't have to move around much and really put myself at risk of overheating.

"Just buy it! You're going to be stressed and you're going to need it!"

"But can't *you* give me a neck rub?" I asked, turning my face away from the wheel spinning on the computer screen. I looked at my husband, sweating away on the dingy slipcover stretched across the minimalist sofa. I'm sure the cloth must have been white at one time, but prolonged use by sweaty, sticky bodies had rendered it a dusty cream.

"What?" he yelled. He could hear me about as well as I could hear him with the swamp cooler blaring profusely. The monstrosity squeaked and groaned as it struggled, miserably, to cool the inside of the room. A glorified dust-blower, it did little to diminish the sweltering heat. It seemed to be better at blowing hot air around than it was at actually fulfilling its intended purpose. I rolled my eyes and leaned over to turn off the beast emerging from the window next to my chair.

"Can't you give me a neck rub every once in a while?" I asked, a little too loudly. With the swamp cooler running, I had grown accustomed to shouting.

"There's only so much I can do," my husband replied at an acceptable yet entirely audible decibel. It was so much easier to carry on a conversation without the loud drone buzzing in the background. "I'm not sure I would be of much help. Besides, between the move and starting your new job, you're going to need it!" He raised his eyebrows with a look that said that he knew what he was talking about, and if I would put my own stubbornness aside, I would arrive at that realization.

"But I don't want to spend the money!" I complained. Sure, the website was offering an exceptional deal on a service that

STRESS SIZE

I actually needed, but still, it cost money. Money that I didn't want to spend.

"Nicole, I'm telling you, you're going to need it!" Raleigh warned. I didn't think it was possible with the intensity of the glare he was giving me, but he raised his eyebrows even higher to emphasize his point.

"Ugh!" I groaned. Even the smallest of decisions seemed to turn into impossible issues with me. I rubbed out some of the numbness in my arm as I contemplated the situation. It was too hot to think clearly. The wobbly wicker chair creaked as I shifted my weight. Skin slicked with sweat pulsed from the fresh impression left by the cross-hatched pattern of the seat. I clawed at the resulting itch, blemishing the already tender skin with bright pink streaks. My pain flared up as I settled back into the wicker chair, still trying to make up my mind.

Raleigh was right, as usual, but I couldn't get past the cost. Twenty-nine dollars was an unbeatable price for an hour of luxury, but it was twenty-nine dollars of my hard-earned money. And for what? For a fleeting feeling of tranquility that would slip away with the inevitable exertion of my muscles? No amount of massage therapy, relaxation techniques, or other health and wellness voodoo could ever truly ease my pain. There were too many toxins built up in my system for anything less than hard drugs or prescription painkillers to at least trick my body into thinking that I had finally found a cure. Alternative medicine was a waste of my time and the cash I worked so hard for.

And yet, the offer tempted me. Nearly a year had passed since I had last allowed myself to be pampered, and that was only because I received a trip to the spa as a gift from Raleigh. Since then, I had endured my final semester of school, numerous health concerns and disappointing trips to the doctor, and the last-minute subleasing of a decrepit house deprived of adequate air conditioning. My muscles ached and there were so many tension knots in my neck that it was visibly swollen, not to mention tender to the touch. Wouldn't that twenty-nine dollars be worth it to not have my body holding on to all that stress, if even for a short while?

"I'll only do it if I get the discount," I concluded. That was fair enough. If I could luck out and get the discount to satisfy my incessant frugality, it was surely a sign from the heavens that I needed to spend more time and money on myself. I clicked the button and watched the green wheel whirl on the screen. The promotional mascot, a comically misshapen face with enlarged and exaggerated features, turned round and round and upside down in the center of the wheel as it spun. The spinning slowed, inching toward the desired discount until it stopped. A new page popped up and suddenly, the room erupted in electronic cheers.

"I won!" I cried, nearly leaping from my sweaty seat. "I won the ten-dollar discount!" I couldn't believe it—only nineteen dollars for an hour of healing. Such a deal was unheard of, impossible. Probably even illegal. Nobody should be able to get a massage that cheap. It was crazy.

"No way!" my husband exclaimed. He smiled a big, toothy grin as he shared in my excitement. "That's amazing! It's destiny. Now you have no excuse!" He probably thought I should have listened to him in the first place, but I was glad I held out for an even better deal. Sure, my stubbornness was difficult to deal with, but my compulsive thriftiness almost always paid off.

"I guess not!" I agreed. "The Universe must have known how much I needed a neck rub," I joked. It couldn't have been divine intervention. Things like winning a discount from an electronically generated wheel were completely random, a matter of chance. The powers that be were too busy dealing with more important issues, like world disasters or something, to directly affect my life. Miracles didn't happen to everyday people like me.

Raleigh saw the wheels turning in my mind as I stared blankly into space. "If you're still concerned about the cost," he said, "you can always wait until you're really stressed before you use it. You know, to make it last longer."

With my mind focused on the apparent absence of the Divine in my stressed out and tightly scheduled life, that wasn't what I was thinking about, but I appreciated the suggestion nonetheless. "That's true," I agreed, keeping my true thoughts to myself.

After a few more clicks, I was the proud new owner of a voucher for a sixty-minute Swedish massage. I braved the obstacle course in the living room to print out my promise of pampering.

"It's kind of too bad I can't use it now," I sighed as I returned to my makeshift workstation, laptop and voucher in hand. "This whole move is stressing me out!"

The oversized oven of a living room, piled to the ceiling with big, heavy boxes, was fraying my nerves. Newspapers, Sharpies, scissors, and rolls of tape scattered on the floor made navigation a nightmare. We were only a few days away from our big move to Denver and there was still so much to be done. I was a wreck trying to get all of the packing done and the moving details squared away. Raleigh, who was focused on grading the last of his students' final exams, tried to help when he could, but I wanted each task to be completed a certain way and I didn't trust him to do things right. I took it upon myself to do everything, on my own and to my own detriment.

"It'll be fine, honey," Raleigh murmured in response to my concern. "Just wait." He paused, reflecting upon the dream that was slowly being realized. "We'll move, we'll get all settled into our new place, you'll start working in your new position—it'll be great!"

It would be great, but it would still be stressful. "Yeah, that's true," I said, attempting to cast my concerns aside. "I wish it could be like, two weeks from now and we were already all moved in. I am not looking forward to that sixteen-hour drive!"

"It's going to be tough, especially with the cats in the car, but it'll be okay. We'll take breaks and we'll have the walkie-talkies to stay in touch."

I sighed and wiped some of the sweat from my legs. The drive was going to be long, but at least the ordeal would be organized. I had compiled a list of every possible stopping point between Tucson and Denver, complete with distances in miles and estimated arrival times in minutes. That way, we would always know how far away we were from an anticipated potty break or snack session. The itinerary was neatly tucked away in an accordion folder to be kept close at hand, along with our rental truck information, hotel reservation for our overnight stay in Albuquerque, leasing application for our new apartment, and confirmation numbers for our new internet service and utilities. I had even printed out instructions for setting up the modem and wireless router to ensure there wouldn't be any gaps in our connectivity. I had everything we needed.

Our new life in Denver was so well planned that it included a spreadsheet detailing my future pay dates, anticipated earnings, and estimated contributions to our savings account. I knew exactly how much money we could spend on gas, groceries, rent, and utilities each month, as well as how often we could afford to eat out or withdraw money for discretionary spending. The rental house may not have been completely packed, but I was prepared for every other possible situation, financial or otherwise.

STRESS SIZE

Not too bad for a girl who had recently graduated from college. No debt, no bills, and the promise of a lucrative career with excellent benefits. Scrimping and scraping would no longer be necessary—my new job would provide us with the financial stability I so desperately craved. I could finally relax and release my worries. I could revel in my newfound sense of security.

Chapter 2

We planned on getting an early start on moving day to beat the heat. What we didn't plan on was forgetting to set the alarm. After a long night of packing, we woke up at seven o'clock instead of five. By the time we got dressed, ate a hearty breakfast of leftover frozen pizza, and packed the last of our belongings into the truck, it was nearly nine. It was still early in the morning, but not so early that the Arizona sun hadn't stolen the sky and made a martyr of the previously cooler temperature.

"The cats are going to be crying ..." my husband envisioned, shaking his shirt to evaporate some of the sweat from his body. We had made our final sweep of the house to make sure we had cleared out all our belongings. We were now convening in the dirt driveway.

"The cats?!" I exclaimed. "I'm the one who's going to be crying! You know I have to eat or pee every half hour!" Sitting in a car for several hours at a time with two crying cats, with no access to facilities or food, was going to be torture.

"Yeah, I know." Raleigh rolled his eyes. Having been together for nearly four years, he had grown accustomed to my frighteningly frequent meals and urination, but that didn't make my behavior any less inconvenient or annoying. "But for your information, we won't get to stop for very long—the cats will get too hot in the car."

STRESS SIZE

My eyes widened. We hadn't even left yet and I could already feel the emptiness in my stomach and the pressure in my bladder. This drive was going to be the death of me.

"Well, I guess I'll have to deal with it," I muttered. I didn't really have a choice. "Let's try and stay calm and remember that we love each other."

"I'll be calm. Are *you* going to be calm?" Raleigh asked. He knew that I had the patience of a ticking time bomb and the worry of a fat, juicy wart.

"Probably not," I said, wrinkling my nose. Imagined scenes of me freaking out, as per usual, came into mind. I knew it wouldn't take much for those visions to become a reality. But it was getting late and it was time to get going. "Do you have your walkie-talkie?" I asked.

"Yes."

"Extra batteries?" I needed to ensure he had everything he needed, or could ever possibly need, stowed away in the cabin of the truck. I had enough worrying to do without having to think about whether Raleigh had remembered everything on the lengthy list of essential supplies.

"Yes," he said, firmly.

"Toolbox with moving gloves and first aid kit?"

"Yes." Raleigh fidgeted in frustration. I could tell from his brisk tone of his voice that he was starting to get annoyed. But that was too bad—I had to double-check. It was for his own good, and for my peace of mind.

"Map?"

"Yes."

"Itinerary?"

"Yes." His patience was running out. I knew I had to hurry.

"Cell phone? Wallet? Keys? Chapstick??" I blurted quickly,

summing up the last of the supplies that I thought he might need.

"Yes, yes, yes, and yes!" Raleigh yelled. "Can we go already?"

"Okay, fine!" I finally let up. "I love you!"

"I love you, too," Raleigh said with a quick kiss.

He climbed into the cabin of the fourteen-foot moving truck and shot me a smile. He was so high up in that big truck that he barely knew how to drive. I smiled back, albeit nervously, and stepped into our dust-encrusted sedan. Armed with my walkie-talkie, the accordion folder, several bottles of water, and what I hoped would be enough snacks, I was as ready as I would ever be to embark on my journey into the unknown.

Our two cats cowered in the backseat, bewildered and wide-eyed. They yowled pitifully as I pulled away from the curb. Our tuxedo cat, Julius, quickly realized that being in motion had little effect on his immediate safety. He curled up into a furry ball in the corner and fell asleep. But the black cat, Nero, cried nearly every moment of the drive. He couldn't stand being in the car—the relentless movement terrified him. Only when his incessant meowing rendered him unconscious was it finally quiet in the car.

I then realized that the racket provided a much-needed distraction. Without the howling to keep my thoughts occupied, my mind wandered.

Were we crazy to pursue such an endeavor? Nobody packed up all their belongings and traveled nearly a thousand miles to a city they'd never even seen before. No friends, no family, not even an acquaintance would be there to await our arrival. For all we knew, we could be putting our faith in a forsaken city. We could end up in a shack in the worst part of town, or worse, fall victim to a senseless crime. How could we be so sure we would be safe and secure when there wasn't anyone there to show us the ropes?

But I had done all the research: analyzed the apartment rentals based on price and size, investigated the crime rates and types of crimes committed, surveyed the surrounding amenities, and determined what we could comfortably afford without sacrificing our safety or the leisure activities to which we had grown accustomed. Surely that would be enough to ensure our happiness. What more could we possibly have to worry about?

When only a few months ago we were both graduating from school and I realized our time in Tucson was coming to an end, I panicked. Sure, I was working part-time as a retail associate, and Raleigh as a teaching assistant at the university, but all that was temporary. It was time to move on, but we didn't know where to go or how to get there. Moving required money, which after four years of scrounging to skirt by without accumulating student loans or debt, we simply didn't have.

We were stuck. That was, we were stuck until I discovered a way out. My manager had been urging me to apply for the company's college recruiting program, which would enable me to skip several steps on the career ladder to jump straight into a management role. I had been avoiding her for months because I didn't really want to work for the company forever, let alone in an authoritative capacity. But with my bachelor of fine arts degree in hand and not using it to get a better job, I became bitter—especially when the first of the college recruits stepped into the store for their six weeks of intensive training.

That should be me, I muttered to myself as I sorted through the mountain of clothes a customer had left abandoned in her cart. *I could totally be an assistant manager.* I was just as qualified, if not more so, as they were for the management position. I was definitely organized and controlling enough.

By the end of the week, my envy had seized control of my

common sense. I sat down with my manager and asked if there was still time to apply for the training program. Unfortunately, the deadline for that particular round of training had passed, but the corporate office was always accepting applications for future training groups. That night, I put together an impressive resume and cover letter. As I sent it off into cyberspace, I hoped that all of my underpaid efforts would finally pay off.

They did.

Shortly thereafter, I received a reply—corporate was interested in having me join their management team. I would just need to complete a few phone interviews with the zone representatives. Easy enough. I wouldn't even have to get dressed for the occasion.

But that still didn't solve the issue of where we were going to live. There were stores all over the country. I could have my pick of any of the finest cities across the nation. But merely taking the plunge to apply for the position had been stressful enough. How could I settle on one city when there were hundreds to choose from?

I sought out Raleigh's opinion. During one of our late-night walks (it was far too hot to venture outside during the day), I asked him where he wanted to go.

"Costa Rica!" he exclaimed. As a Spanish instructor and linguist, he had always dreamed of living abroad.

"That's not an option, silly. We don't have any stores there. Besides, that's too far." Moving out of state would be challenging enough. Moving out of the country would be flat-out crazy.

"Well, you asked me where I wanted to go," he said, somewhat hurt that I had immediately dismissed his desires.

"In the United States!" I clarified

"Then you need to be more specific!"

"Okay, fine. So, where in the *United States* do you want to go?"

"I don't know," he replied. He thought for a moment, and then asked, "I'd need to think about this. Can we talk about this later?"

I didn't have time to mess around. I had waited long enough for the rest of our lives to fall into place. "I have my phone interview tomorrow and they're probably going to ask me where I'm planning to relocate."

"So, they can't hire you now and have you decide later?" That possibility certainly would have postponed my concern, but it wasn't practical.

"No," I answered matter-of-factly. He didn't seem to pick up on the urgency of the situation. I was obviously going to have to spell it all out for him. "They have to know where to place me. They have to make sure that there's a need for me in the market. They might even have to move other managers around to make room for me in a particular store if they think it will be a good fit."

"They can do that?" he asked. "That hardly seems fair to the other managers if they're being shoved out of their own store." It wasn't fair, but it was beyond my control.

"They're a nationwide company with a thousand locations," I replied. "They can pretty much do whatever they want."

Raleigh was silent as he reflected upon the questionable business practices of the company I was about to entrust with the rest of my working life.

"So, where do you want to go?" I asked again when I thought he had pondered for long enough. "If you could live anywhere in the country, where would you go?"

"Well, I hadn't really thought about it," he admitted.

"What do you mean you hadn't thought about it?" I squealed, astonished. Here I was, trying to plan out our lives together, and he hadn't even given our future a passing thought. "Did you think we were going to live here forever?"

"Well, no, but it's kind of hard to think about the future when you're writing papers, teaching classes, and taking finals." The way he rattled off his responsibilities, I could tell that the conversation could easily turn into a contest of who was the busiest bee.

Raleigh didn't see me roll my eyes in the darkness. Between spending nearly thirty hours a week on school commitments, working as a retail associate for another fifteen, and squeezing in at least ten extra hours at the studio on the weekends to complete my art projects, I was just as busy as he was, if not more. Somehow that didn't stop me from finding the time to cook meals, clean the house, and think about the future. Being busy was not a sufficient excuse for ignoring important issues.

But I bit my bitter tongue and steered the discussion back on track. "I know my hometown is too small, and we want to get out of Arizona anyway, but what about moving to Houston to be near your family?"

"No," Raleigh said firmly, considering the case closed. "I am *not* moving to Houston." He declared this with such absolute resolution that I knew I had to pry into the matter further. I had offered up a solution to a problem he hadn't even remotely considered, yet he immediately shot down my proposal. I needed answers.

"Why not?" I asked with as much innocence as I could muster in my aggravated state. "What's wrong with Houston?"

"First of all, it's too hot there."

"It's too hot *here!*" I exclaimed. Had he not spent the past two or three months sweating on a stranger's sofa while we subleased, melting away as the swamp cooler failed miserably to eliminate the sweltering heat inside our subleased home? For a man with such limited options in a crunched timeframe, he wasn't making any sense.

STRESS SIZE

"Yeah, so take this heat, add some humidity, and you have Houston," Raleigh retorted.

"I don't believe you!" I declared, shaking my head in the dark. The motion was more for my own satisfaction and emphasis than for his viewing. "We were there for Christmas and the weather was fine."

"That was in the *winter*," he explained. "You've never been to Houston in the summer."

He had a point. "But I grew up in California," I continued to reason. "I can handle a little humidity."

"It's not just a little humidity. It's a lot of humidity. We'll be miserable."

I wanted to protest, but I had run out of reasonable arguments. The sweat collecting on my skin, despite the sun having set several hours before, assured me that he was right. My tolerance for heat was minimal at best, excruciating for anyone misfortunate enough to be around me at worst. Getting overheated made me cranky. Adding humidity into the mix would have fueled the already blazing fire.

"Well, fine." I finally muttered. Another win for Raleigh. "But that's not really a good enough reason."

"Well, it's not the only reason," he said.

"Then give me another reason!" I needed something more than some uncomfortable weather to keep me from moving to a place that could offer us reasonable hope of seeing our home-owning dreams quickly realized. From what I had encountered during our last visit over winter break, real estate was cheap, ready and waiting for the picking. Not only that, but the houses were obscenely huge. The price per square foot was a remarkable deal, virtually unbeatable by that of any other region in the country. With me working full-time in a high-paying position, we could afford the minimum down payment for a big fancy house in less than a year.

Raleigh inhaled deeply, preparing himself for his confession. "I don't want to live that close to my family," he breathed.

Well, *that* was unexpected. He had spent the last six years away from home, first, to get his undergraduate degree, and then, to pursue his master's degree as I finished my own undergraduate coursework at the university. With money being so tight, he rarely visited his family, maybe once a year now that we were married and living on our own. I thought for sure he'd be willing to brave the hot and sticky weather simply to be closer to home.

"They're your *family!*" I exclaimed. "How could you not want to live close to them?"

"I love my family," he replied. "And I know you do too. But if we live in the same city as them, they'll be over all the time, wanting to help us out. We'll never get to see what it's like to make it on our own."

"We've been on our own for two years," I stated, "and it *sucks*." Living off surplus scholarship funds, a modest graduate assistant stipend, and minimum wage was not the ideal way to start off a marriage. Between struggling to make ends meet and trying to adjust to living in such close quarters with another person (all while taking on an overbooked course load of advanced studio classes), I had already had enough. With much of my future still in flux, I needed some semblance of stability. I needed the kind of comfort that only being surrounded by my family could provide, and the occasional holiday visit wasn't going to cut it.

By the way Raleigh exclaimed, he was hurt by my remark. "Hey! It hasn't been that bad. We're not on the streets or starving or anything. We're doing okay. And besides, all this struggling has only made us stronger."

My eyes rolled, again. I was sick of struggling. I didn't care if it made me stronger. I wanted things to be easy for a change. But I supposed there was some kernel of truth in what he was saying. And, more than I appreciated that realization, I was tired of arguing with him. I stopped pressing the issue.

"Okay, fine," I sighed. "So, if that's the case, where do you see yourself living for the next several years?"

He thought for a moment and then replied, "Colorado sounds nice."

"Colorado?" I asked, eyebrows arched. The suggestion seemed a little out of the ordinary. He had mentioned that place before, but only in passing. I didn't take his whims very seriously. "Have you ever even been to Colorado?"

"Well, no," he admitted.

"So why do you want to move there?" Again, I couldn't accept what he had said at face value. I needed answers.

"It sounds nice."

"That's an awful long move to a place that 'just sounds nice.' What if you don't like it?"

"I'll like it!" he insisted.

"Yeah, but how do you *know*?"

"I just do."

"That doesn't make any sense! You haven't even been there!" The man was talking crazy. People didn't pick up and move to a place that they hadn't even seen.

"I know I'm going to like it."

He had obviously made up his mind. The most I could do at that point was boil the situation down to some specifics. "So, where in Colorado were you thinking?" We'd narrowed down our relocation possibilities to a single state. I at least wanted to pinpoint a particular city before ending the conversation. The actual store I would be working in could be left up to the company.

"I don't know," Raleigh replied. "Denver, maybe."

"Are you sure?" These were life-changing decisions we were making here during our brisk walk in the dark. He needed to be absolutely sure before I went off and reported my top choice to the human resources director during my phone interview the next day.

"Yeah, why not?"

"Because they're going to ask me where we want to move, and I want to be able to tell them with absolute certainty."

"So tell them!"

"But that's crazy! Neither of us has even been there!" Were we really going to take such a blind leap of faith, no questions asked?

"Well, we don't want to stay here, and we've already established that we can't move to Houston, and Kingman is out of the question, so anywhere we go is going to be someplace we've never been to before." He had a point, but his words didn't make me feel much better.

By that time, we had completed our walk around the unlit neighborhood and returned to the house. We fought off the bugs swarming around the porch light as we entered the front door. Standing under the light, Raleigh caught a glimpse my lips pursed in a pronounced pout. "We'll have to trust that everything will be okay."

"But I can't," I whispered, on the verge of tears. I wanted to be in complete control of everything in my life. That was the only way my mind could be at ease—knowing everything was planned out and accounted for. But as it stood, there were too many variables, too many important issues left up to chance. I couldn't rest when faced with the unknown.

"But you will," he assured me. He flicked on a light in the foyer and looked deep into my eyes. He caressed my arm in an effort to console me. "You need to stop worrying. Everything is going to be okay."

For a moment, I almost believed him.

Chapter 3

THE REPETITION OF *SHRUB, DIRT, SHRUB* MADE THE DRIVE monotonous, and I found myself playing orchestral music obnoxiously loudly to avoid falling asleep. But even with complicated piano concertos pounding in my ears, I still found space in my brain to worry. I hashed out every scenario that could possibly arise as we adjusted to our new life in a strange city, anticipating every possible course of action for any given situation. I even organized the imagined issues from least likely to most likely, from tolerable to completely unbearable and possibly life-ending.

When I finished with that, I went through the entire list again, in order, just to make sure I had it all straightened out. I was doing pretty well with that until Nero arose from his self-inflicted stupor and launched into another boisterous round of meowing. Annoying, but a sufficient and appreciated distraction.

With me leading the way and Raleigh trailing behind, we stopped every hour or two—Raleigh to stretch his legs, and me to pee. Raleigh and I topped off our tanks at a generic gas station past the New Mexico border. I, of course, stashed the receipts safely away in my accordion folder. Tax write-offs for the job-related move. Every little bit helped. We then stopped briefly for lunch at a sandwich shop a little farther down the road.

"Will the cats be okay with the windows down?" I asked Raleigh, stretching my arms to the sky and out to the sides. The fresh air was invigorating, and it was nice to step out of the sedan and stretch out my legs. I had been abusing the cruise control and didn't need to keep my foot on the gas, but I could only tolerate sitting in a cramped space for so long.

"You'd better hope so," Raleigh replied, doing full-on lunges in the dusty parking lot to work out the cramps in his legs. His driving situation was not nearly as fortunate as mine since the rental truck was not equipped with cruise control. He had to have his foot pressed to the pedal at all times, sometimes all the way down to the floorboard, to keep that big heavy beast moving. I'd nearly lost him on the freeway a couple of times because he had a hard time accelerating uphill. I had to break my coasting streak to slow down and let him catch up.

"I can only open the windows a crack. Otherwise, the cats might jump out." They were probably too terrified to attempt an escape in the middle of nowhere, but I didn't want to take any chances.

At the higher elevation, the air was slightly cooler than that of our now former hometown. It was still hot, and possibly dangerous for the cats to stay in the car, but an extended rest would have been appreciated. Raleigh thought for a moment and then said, "I think we should eat on the road. I don't want to come out and find the cats died in the car because they got too hot."

I sighed. Having only made it through the first fourth of our trip, we still had a long drive ahead of us. The next stretch was marked by a mess of mustard and other sandwich fixings as I attempted to eat and drive at the same time. The sonatas Raleigh had compiled were somewhat soothing, but Nero's crying, now interrupted by the perplexed yelps of his previously placid playmate, grated on my nerves. I could hardly keep myself from flinging my turkey sandwich at him in frustration.

I was relieved when we finally reached the halfway point of

our trek—a franchise hotel in Albuquerque. We checked in and unloaded our suitcases, the cats, and their litter box before venturing into town. We had a gift card for a familiar restaurant, and, of course, a printout of a street map complete with directions. I had even obtained directions to a nearby shopping mall so we would have somewhere to relax after dinner.

I was tired and hungry, but there's always that question of what to eat. Having already consumed half a personal pizza for breakfast and a turkey sandwich on honey wheat with the works for lunch, I had more than exhausted my carbohydrate limit for the day. I stared at the menu, stomach aching and mind muddled. Everything looked good, and nothing looked good, all at the same time.

"Just pick something," my husband pleaded. He had already made up his mind several minutes before and was ready to place his order.

"I can't!" I cried. There were too many choices, too many tempting calories. But I couldn't eat whatever I wanted. My meals had to be well thought out, meaningful and nourishing. Every calorie counted. "Nothing sounds good," I complained. I flipped through the menu for the third or fourth time, eyeing each of the meticulously staged shots of delicious yet incredibly fattening meals.

"What are you craving?" Raleigh asked. He rattled off a bunch of options, only adding to my confusion. I couldn't concentrate when he was talking to me. I shushed him and he rolled his eyes.

"I don't know," I finally answered. "I could almost go for a salad." Maybe.

"So, order a salad."

"But it's such a waste. It's like, ten dollars for a heap of lettuce." I could get a whole head of lettuce at the store for a dollar, and all the toppings for a couple more. All that would yield a whole week's worth of salads, and here I was, considering squandering a chunk of change on a meal I couldn't even take to go because it would wilt.

"But it's a *gift card*. It's like getting the food for free." He squinted his eyes at me, attempting to understand my rationale, but not fully comprehending the economics of the situation. His carefree mind didn't work the way my overly conscientious one did.

"I don't care if it's a gift card," I asserted. "It's still a waste."

"Then get something else."

"But anything else is too fatty!" The menu featured a wide array of thick, creamy soups, overstuffed sandwiches, and juicy cheeseburgers accompanied by piping hot french fries. Each of the entrées was a nightmare for a careful calorie consumer. There was very little offered in the way of healthy alternatives. "I don't want all those calories!"

"Seriously. Pick something," Raleigh hissed, his patience wearing thin. "The waitress is coming back and I want to be able to place my order."

I looked up to see the young woman who had taken our drink order (waters, of course, because those were cheaper than soft drinks) weaving her way through the restaurant as she returned to our table. Now the pressure was really on. I flipped through the menu again, now more furiously than ever, as I went into panic mode. Within moments the waitress arrived, all smiles. "May I take your order?" she asked.

She was perky, upbeat, and friendly. She possessed all the customer-centric qualities I could possibly hope for in a waitress. But what she didn't realize was that no, she couldn't take my order because I didn't even know what I wanted to order, and I couldn't very well make a decision now that she was standing there watching me. Between her awaiting my reply, and Raleigh glaring at me from across the booth, it was too much pressure.

"I'm sorry," I replied, still gripping the menu. "I need a few more minutes."

"No problem," she said. "I'll be back in a few." She sauntered off to assist a customer who could actually be helped, leaving me to mull over the menu for yet another round.

Raleigh rolled his eyes and slapped his menu onto the table. He crossed his arms indignantly as I reluctantly settled on a salad topped with crispy breaded chicken. Hearty enough to warrant the cost, but not so unhealthy that my caloric intake for the day would suffer immensely. He was very much relieved when the waitress returned and we finally placed our order.

I must have been hungrier than I thought because I devoured every last shred of lettuce and chicken on my plate. I even wiped up the crumbs with my finger, being sure to include the last traces of creamy salad dressing. When I had all but licked the plate clean, I sat back in my seat, satisfied.

The waitress returned and asked if we would like a bag to take home the chips that had accompanied my husband's meal. I looked at the plastic basket on the table, which, as the second round, was still piled high with tortilla chips. Raleigh, in all of his hunger and frustration, had quickly consumed the first batch and didn't refuse the second when the waitress brought it by without even being asked. I didn't really want the chips but, not wanting to be wasteful, I told her that would be fine. She left and came back with a large plastic bag bursting with a fresh batch.

My eyes widened. I had been expecting an empty paper bag to take home what we already had. Had I known she was going to bring us more, I probably would have declined her offer. What were we going to do with so many chips? I didn't even want them in the first place!

Raleigh thanked the waitress, and, sensing my concern, said, "You'll want some when we're on the road."

"I'm not eating those," I said firmly. There was no way. There were way too many. The chips in that bag could feed a small country.

"You're going to want them," he said, half teasing, half serious. We tipped the waitress and left, arms loaded with chips and a side of salsa.

The sun settled into the sky as the day crept into early evening. We proceeded to the nearby shopping mall, but only after getting lost with only our printed directions to guide us.

We were exhausted by the time we arrived at the mall. It had been a long day, but there wasn't anything to do at the hotel except watch TV. Anticipating another long drive the next day, we at least wanted to stretch our legs for a while. Staring at store displays was better than being bored senseless in an unfamiliar room.

As we walked past the various windows displaying designer goods, we suddenly smelled the sweet scent of cinnamon wafting in the air. My eyes widened with terror. I had smelled that scent before, and it meant trouble. Something dangerous was baking in a nearby corner in the mall, and with its aroma embedded in Raleigh's nostrils, I knew what would happen next.

"Do you smell what I smell?" Raleigh asked excitedly. His masculine features transformed into a picture of boyish delight at the prospect of a treat.

Cinnamon buns.

"I'm getting one," he declared, quickening his pace with a new-found destination in mind.

"Raleigh, don't!" I pleaded. I needed to stop him before he reached the counter and made a terrible mistake.

"Why not?" he asked, stopping in his tracks. The other patrons of the mall strolled past us as we stood in the middle of the walkway. I motioned for us to move off to the side.

"Because I don't want one," I replied.

"But *I* want one."

"Then use your own money."

"But that's not fair," he whined.

"How is that not fair? You're the one who wants one, so you should have to use your own money." It made sense to me. We were each allotted a certain amount of money from each paycheck for personal spending, no questions asked. The cash withdrawal was typically modest due to our meager earnings, but the amount Raleigh had accrued over the past several weeks was more than enough to pay for the treat he so desperately desired, and many times over at that. There was no reason why he should have to use joint money for the expenditure, especially if he was to be the only one consuming the calorie-laden cinnamon bun.

"Why don't you want any?" he asked.

I thought the reason was obvious, but I went ahead and spelled it out anyway. "Raleigh, we just ate dinner," I reminded him. "I don't need any more calories."

"So I have to suffer because you're on some diet?"

"I'm not on a diet," I contested.

"You're restricting your caloric intake and limiting the types of food you eat. How is that not a diet?"

"It's called being aware of the nutrient density of different types of food," I retorted. He had obviously never taken a course in health and nutrition. I, on the other hand, had taken several.

"Whatever," he scoffed. "Call it whatever you want. It's a diet."

STRESS SIZE

"Raleigh!"

"I'm getting one," he said again. He marched away and was out of sight as he rounded the corner.

"Raleigh, wait!" I chased after him. What should have been a private conversation was becoming an embarrassing spectacle in the middle of the mall. People were beginning to stare at us as we raised our voices.

"What?" he cried, exasperated. I was clearly impeding his mission.

"Can you at least not get the milk?" The cinnamon bun I could probably handle, at least with some coaxing, but the milk was asking for too much. It was bad enough that Raleigh was coercing me into a purchase I wasn't thrilled about. It was worse because he always insisted on having a tall glass of ice-cold milk to accompany his compulsory sweets. His peculiarity would result in expense being piled upon frivolous expense.

"But I need milk," he insisted. "I have to have milk with something sweet." He crossed his arms and shook his head, denying my modest request.

"No, you don't *need* milk. You don't need anything. You *want* milk." A need was something that couldn't be lived without. A want was something that could be lived without. There was clearly a difference. Raleigh could easily live without the milk. He could live without the cinnamon bun, too, but I was at least allowing him that luxury. Why did he have to make things more difficult than they already were?

"Okay, so, I want the milk. What's the big deal?"

The reason should have been obvious, but clearly, I was going to have to explain every last detail of the delicate financial situation. "The big deal is that by the time you get the cinnamon bun and the milk, it's going to be like eight dollars."

"So what?" he asked.

My eyes bulged with frustration. I wanted to grab him by the shoulders to shake some sense into him, even with all the people passing by and possibly watching. How could he not understand? It was a simple matter of subtraction. "So, that's eight dollars less than what we had before."

"It's only eight dollars!" he shouted. He still didn't get it.

Eight dollars probably didn't seem like much money to him, but he wasn't the one paying the bills and planning out our finances. He didn't see how quickly money seemed to disappear, especially when it was spent so carelessly on unnecessary commodities like cinnamon buns. He didn't realize that sure, it's only eight dollars now, but eight dollars adds up when sooner or later (most likely sooner), he would see something else that he capriciously wanted and would buy that too. Next thing you know, I would be looking over the banking statement and discover he'd spent thirty or forty dollars on useless junk. That was half a week's worth of groceries or a full tank of gas. There were so many better things, more important things, on which we could be spending our precious money. "But what if I need that eight dollars later?"

"Nicole, you're being ridiculous," he said. He didn't see all the reasoning behind my insistence that he not make the purchase. "I'm getting the cinnamon bun. And I'm getting the milk. You can either enjoy some with me or not, but I'm getting it."

I almost cried as he handed over his debit card and charged seven dollars to our account. A dollar less than I had anticipated, but seven dollars more than I wanted to spend. I continued to pout as Raleigh savored the sugary sweetness of the steaming cinnamon bun.

"Enjoy it," I said bitterly. "This is the last cinnamon bun you're going to get with joint money. If you want another one, you'll have to buy it yourself." Raleigh pretended to ignore me and smacked his lips with gusto as he consumed a large, sticky bite of the cinnamon bun dripping with pecans and thick, creamy frosting.

After Raleigh had devoured the roll, we finished our stroll around the mall in silence and returned to the hotel. We hadn't fed the cats that morning since we didn't know how their sensitive stomachs would handle the constant motion during the long drive. Once back in the room, we attempted to feed them a modest portion of kibble, but in their fright of the unfamiliar, they refused to eat. The way they were behaving, they seemed to be as terrified as I was of the unknown.

Poor kitties, I thought. *They're just like me.*

The next day we woke up early, right on schedule. We scarfed down a continental breakfast of buttered toast in the hotel lobby, checked out, and continued on to the second half our journey. Nero cried, Julius slept, and I replayed all the CDs at my disposal at an obnoxious decibel to keep myself from drifting off.

The second half of the drive would have been a complete repeat of the day before had it not been for the change in scenery. Now climbing at a steady grade as we scaled the mountains of New Mexico, the plant life was much more vibrant and green than what we had left in the dry desert valley. Even in the middle of summer, tall trees stood proud and wildflowers flourished. It was a welcome sight, a much-needed visual delight.

Raleigh and I celebrated over the walkie-talkies when we finally crossed the border into Colorado. We were still a long way from our final destination, but at least we were in the right state. With most of our drive finally behind us, we stopped for lunch in a small mountain town at a café tucked inside the convenience store that accompanied the only gas station for miles.

At the considerably higher elevation, the air was almost cold. We weren't prepared for the cooler weather wearing shorts and T-shirts, but with all the heat we had endured in the past few years, we found the briskness to be refreshing. We cracked the windows and left the cats in the car knowing they would be safe.

Inside the convenience store, we were bombarded with a plethora of snacks and sweets on the shelves. Raleigh, famished after our scant breakfast, drooled over every item on the café menu. Soups, salads, sandwiches. Cookies, candies, and chocolates. The café even had some specialty local items for sale, like fresh fruit, trail mix, and honey.

He wanted a little bit of everything. But of course, each item was either too expensive or laden with calories. We weren't going to strike a balance between a good deal and a nutritious meal, not in the middle of nowhere.

"What about a salad?" Raleigh suggested after I had shot down his proposal of an oversized medley. Obtaining a taste of each treat was simply not plausible with a tight budget.

"Salads are expensive," I replied. We had already had this same discussion the night before, but apparently the matter needed to be revisited.

Raleigh understood, and in an effort to avoid rehashing the same old issue, he offered another suggestion. "What if we split a sandwich?"

"I don't want all that bread," I complained, shaking my head. With all the wild suggestions he was throwing out thoughtlessly, he didn't seem to know me at all. Bread was nothing more than a spongy mass of overly packed carbohydrates. It didn't offer any of the nutrients essential for optimal health. It was a waste of calories. I didn't want it.

"You need bread," he asserted. "Bread's good for you."

STRESS SIZE

It wasn't, really, but I wasn't about to dive into a treatise on the finer points of nutrient density in the middle of the convenience store, especially not when our turn was coming up in line and we would need to place our order with the cashier. "I had bread this morning," I reminded him. "I had several pieces of toast, with butter!" Surely, that would be enough to satisfy him and his flawed thinking.

It wasn't. "Have some more," he insisted.

I could have pulled my hair out in frustration. "I've had enough bread for today," I seethed. "I don't want any more."

"Why do you have to be so difficult?" Raleigh sighed. He was as annoyed as I was about my stringent eating habits. He rubbed his temple and chose his next words carefully. "If you don't want a salad, and you don't want a sandwich, what is it you're craving?"

"Nothing, really."

"Nothing? So, out of everything they have, there isn't one thing you'd like to eat?"

I thought for a moment, delving deep into my gut to determine what it was I actually wanted. I attempted to cast all my calorie cares and financial concerns aside to pinpoint what it was that I sincerely, truly craved. "The salad, I guess," I finally answered.

"So then let's split the salad. Then it won't be so expensive. We'll only be sharing the one thing."

That seemed fair, and I was sick of arguing. Ordering lunch had turned into quite the ordeal. If there had been anyone unfortunate enough to be waiting behind us, we would have been holding up the line. "Fine," I exhaled, exasperated. But still, I was concerned. "Will that be enough for you?"

Raleigh tended to have a bigger and more varied appetite than I did. Something as light as a salad probably wouldn't hold him over until we were able to have dinner. We still needed to drive the rest of the way to Denver, stop by the apartment office and sign the lease, drive to the restaurant, place an order, and wait for the food to arrive. All that would take hours.

"Probably not," he answered, "but I'll be fine." I had forgotten Raleigh didn't get cranky when he was hungry. He usually maintained his composure, even on an empty stomach. I, on the other hand, became extremely irritable when famished. Food was the only thing I could think about when I was hungry. Heaven forbid anyone or anything got in the way of me and eating. And there I was, worrying about whether or not Raleigh would stay full while on the road when I was probably the one who was going to get hungry first. Raleigh, while reflecting upon the remaining tasks, and knowing I probably wouldn't make it through the rest of the day without needing a snack, became equally concerned and added, "You're the one I'm worried about."

I was worried, too, but since we'd argued in front of the cashier for a grossly inconsiderate amount of time, we finally ordered the salad and sat down at one of the few tables in the eating area. I attempted and failed to relax as I settled into the cramped seat. My stomach rumbled. My patience was wearing out.

"What's taking so long?" I asked impatiently.

"Nicole, it's only been a few minutes since we ordered," Raleigh reminded me. "They have to make the food, you know. And besides, I think there was someone else ahead of us."

He had a point, but that didn't make the situation any more bearable. I was tired and hungry, and still had a long day ahead of me. The stress was mounting. I could feel the pain pulsing in my neck and shoulders as my worries continued to settle over me. I sighed and stared up at the ceiling. Suddenly, I gasped.

"What?" Raleigh asked, concerned. In my fatigued and famished state, he thought perhaps something was the matter.

"They have exposed beams!" I exclaimed. Dark raw wood ran along the width of the inside of the building, creating a warm, cozy, and inviting interior. There was something charming and rustic about the wood-covered ceiling, even in the middle of a convenience store. I wasn't expecting such an obscure location to contain such a beautiful sight. I was mesmerized.

Raleigh looked up to see what I was staring at. "So?" he asked. He didn't see the beauty in the subtle variations in tone, the cracks in the grain, or the occasional knot or pit. Each piece of wood was slightly imperfect but nonetheless astonishing. Side by side, they created a spectacle.

"I've always wanted exposed beams," I said dreamily. I envisioned my dream home, something cozy with character, yet with plenty of space and enough room for a painting studio. As the encapsulation of rustic charm mixed with a contemporary aesthetic, it would, of course, feature exposed beams. A touch of the exterior in the interior would breathe fresh life into my quiet home.

Raleigh smiled, enjoying my brief moment of happiness. With all the planning and stress, such moments were few and far between. Somehow, even taking three or four art classes at a time, my wild imagination had begun to slow down, and eventually it came to a complete stop. I had let reason win in the battle between practicality and playfulness. I had all but lost my whimsical sense of spirit.

"Maybe we'll have exposed beams someday," he said, daring me to dream.

"I sure hope so," I replied.

I thought, then, of what our living situation had been like. For the first two years of our marriage, we had lived in an undersized one-bedroom apartment off campus. We were still in school then, and between writing papers, painting pictures, and parenting two cats, the modest 500-square-foot space quickly became even smaller. The 750 square feet of our new, oversized one-bedroom abode in Denver would be a refreshing change of scene.

The two-bedroom 950-square-foot house we had subleased for the summer was spacious enough, but the lodging had been arranged at the last minute and was so temporary that we hadn't even unpacked most of our belongings. It was strange, trying to live our lives amidst the furniture and possessions of a complete stranger. Unnerving, really. Even more so when we discovered dead flies in the freezer and dozens of half-empty jars of expired food in the fridge. With all these idiosyncrasies, the place didn't feel like home.

But there was nothing else we could have done. When the lease at our apartment ended and we didn't want to commit to another full year in Tucson, we didn't really see another option. Subleasing afforded us the opportunity to get our bearings and figure things out without having to sign a contract.

It worked out, too, because Raleigh was offered a part-time teaching position at the university for the summer session and I was able to apply for and obtain my promotion with the company. With the two of us working that summer, we were barely able to save up enough money to finally leave Tucson behind.

Now we were on the road, our sights set on an apartment we had never even seen in person before. We had only looked at images on the internet, mentally piecing the pictures together to get an idea of what it really looked like. Of course, models always make the apartment appear more pristine than the actual product, but I hoped for the best. I had to. Otherwise, my fragile mental state would disintegrate.

Sure, we could have made a trip out to the unfamiliar city to check it out and make sure that's where we really wanted to settle down. Should have, really. But the cost was a prohibitive concern. Somehow it made more sense to take the plunge rather than second-guess our impulsive decision. And besides, that's what intensive internet-based research was for. How could anything possibly go wrong when I had planned everything out?

Taking comfort in my own planning and organizing skills, my anxiety subsided somewhat. I nestled my tired body into the hard seat and rested as I waited for the food. We shared the salad once it arrived, but only after heatedly discussing the amount of dressing with which to drench it. I preferred a light dousing. Raleigh wanted a deluge. We finally settled on some amount in between.

Once we had finished, I told Raleigh I was going to check on the cats before we headed back out. This was the first time we had left them alone in the car for more than a couple of minutes. As I peeked through the back window of the car, I nearly panicked when I couldn't find Nero. There was no way he could have slipped through one of the cracks in the windows, at least not without hurting himself. Could he have crept out when I had opened the door to venture out to the café? As I soon discovered, he had somehow squeezed himself under the passenger seat, as if hiding would somehow protect him from the unknown.

I gently pulled out his tense body from underneath the seat and scratched his jet-black head. He immediately relaxed, squinting his eyes half-closed in unquestioning acceptance of my comforting attention. I sighed, relieved he was not out wandering the wilderness. He wasn't as smart, or as brave, as his adoptive brother Julius and wouldn't last long in the wild. He was a delicate creature, sensitive and terrified of change. Just like me.

"Silly, Nero," I said, stroking his fur. He shed excessively when frightened, and his fur came out in tufts. He didn't seem to mind. "Don't be scared," I whispered. Mostly, the words were for me.

When Nero's fright faded away and he began purring loudly, I nestled him onto the back seat and checked on Julius. He hadn't made a peep the whole morning, so I assumed he was okay. I was horrified to discover he had confined himself to his crate and was sitting behind a sticky pool of his own vomit.

"Poor baby," I cried. He glanced at me pitifully, as though still sick to his stomach. He didn't make a sound as I coaxed him out of the crate, careful not brush his fur against the contents he'd expelled. His hunger had gotten the best of him that morning and he had consumed every last kibble we had set out. He had handled the first half of our journey so well, Raleigh and I didn't think it would be an issue for him to eat before hitting the road again. Unfortunately, we were wrong. Who knew how long he had been stewing in his own regurgitation!

Raleigh, who had been waiting in the cabin of the moving truck, traversed the parking lot to see what all the fuss was about.

"Are you having issues?" he asked.

"Yeah!" I sighed. "I thought I had lost Nero, and now I saw that Julius got sick in the car."

That explained why we hadn't left right away as he was expecting. He examined the mess, which sometime during the drive had dribbled onto the upholstered seat, leaving a thick, crusty stain.

"Gross," he grimaced. He could see now that this was going to be a pain to deal with and would require some time and patience. "What do you need me to do?"

I handed him some of the spare napkins I had stored in the car, and together we cleaned up the mess as best as we could without employing the use of shampoo. We wiped out the pet carrier and emptied the now contaminated water bowl. The cats hadn't

STRESS SIZE

really been drinking the water, but we refilled the vessel with a fresh supply from my own stash anyway. As I repositioned Julius more comfortably in the back seat, he looked up at me with sad, sleepy eyes. I wanted to take away his pain and sickness, but I couldn't. He settled for the comfort of my hand gently stroking his fur and drifted off to sleep.

Not much farther down the road, I began experiencing my own intestinal issues—my stomach began grumbling. It hadn't taken very long for the salad to pass right through my system and for me to get hungry again. Raleigh had been right in asserting that I needed something more substantial than a salad. He was also right in assuming I would turn to the bag of chips after all.

The cooking oil must have gone rancid from sitting in the car, because after eating a small handful of chips, my stomach churned. All I wanted to do was to pull over to the side of the road and spew out the contents of my stomach, but such a reaction was impossible at my high speed. I cast the troublemakers aside and vowed never to eat tortilla chips again. With several more hours of the drive remaining, I stewed in my pain and nausea.

There's nothing quite like suffering in the middle of nowhere. With my stomach tied up in knots, I thought perhaps I was dying. And, much to my dismay, I was miles and miles away from a medical facility, and it would have been impossible to find without some sort of printout or map to guide me. I was stuck, solitary in my suffering.

Eventually, my stomach's cantankerous condition transitioned to mild languish. I was grateful, but that didn't stop me from turning my discomfort into full-blown bitterness. Hadn't I already endured enough bodily dysfunction to last me an entire lifetime?

First there was my missing period. Somehow my clockwork cycle had gone straight from Thanksgiving to Valentine's Day with only a speck of blood in between. I thought perhaps I was pregnant. Not the worst-case scenario, especially with school coming to an end, but not exactly an ideal situation for someone who planned on having a bright and prosperous future. I mentioned the possibility to Raleigh before confirming or disproving my theory, and we reluctantly agreed to accept our fate either way. But as fate would have it, multiple pregnancy tests revealed I wasn't pregnant after all.

The news was bittersweet. I should have been relieved that I wouldn't have to deal with the drama of delivering a baby and trying to figure out how to support it, but I was concerned. I had always been so regular, and I had no idea what was going on with me. My body was changing and I didn't know why.

The doctors at the campus health clinic didn't know why either. One of the physicians had discovered a mild bacterial infection, but nothing that would warrant such a drastic change in my hormonal health. "Sometimes women skip a cycle or two," she suggested with a mildly apologetic smile, "especially if they're stressed."

"I'm not stressed," I retorted with a shiver. My crew cut socks did little to warm my legs, which stuck out from underneath the starchy examination gown. In an effort to warm myself in the chilly examination room, I swung my feet back and forth fervently as they dangled over the edge of the paper-covered table. "And I don't 'skip a cycle,'" I added determinedly. The doctor smiled politely, not quite believing my statement, and left me alone to get dressed and ponder my problems in silence.

Then, there were the sharp chest pains and frequent heart palpitations. I didn't habitually consume caffeine, only occasionally sipped a cup of hot tea, so I thought for sure there was something amiss. I worried that I suffered from congenital heart failure or some other chronic condition. But after conducting a series of tests to monitor the electrical current and rhythm of my heart, the cardiologist couldn't determine the cause of my symptoms.

"It's probably heartburn or acid reflux," she shrugged. "And sometimes the heart skips a beat. It's nothing to worry about." As if the frightening possibility of keeling over from sudden heart failure was nothing to be afraid of.

To make matters more perplexing, there was also the matter of my drastic and unintended weight loss. Within a couple of weeks, I had lost nearly ten pounds. I went from barely being able to squeeze in my jeans to having to invest in a new wardrobe—all without changing my ambitious eating habits.

At first, I didn't mind the unexpected new me. I even adopted a healthier lifestyle, eating a vegetarian diet and getting regular exercise, to maintain my new image. Initially weighing in at nearly 150 pounds at 5'7", I hadn't exactly been overweight, but I had always considered myself to be a little on the robust side of the weight scale. Dropping ten pounds had done wonders for my self-esteem. I wanted to keep it that way.

With Raleigh being a steadfast vegetarian, I had already grown accustomed to a life with very little meat. It wasn't very difficult for me to limit, or even completely cut out, milk, cheese, bread, and other sources of unnecessary calories. The transition to a diet solely comprised of fruits and vegetables was virtually seamless as I focused on foods that were nutrient-dense and could offer me the biggest health impact for the lowest amount of calories.

For a while, I felt great—healthy and reenergized. My persistent fatigue and moderate depression subsided as I began exercising every other day and eating plenty of wholesome, nutritious foods. But somehow even eating such a sparse, healthful diet caused problems. The smallest nibble of fruit would have me doubled over in pain. I tried narrowing down my already limited repertoire of acceptable foods to only vegetables, but to no avail. My stomach couldn't seem to tolerate anything. Yet again, the doctors were stumped.

"Eat some crackers and drink some ginger ale," the so-called specialist stated. And so I did, for a while, until my stomach stopped rejecting the nutritious food I was trying to feed it. Even though eating was no longer an agonizing activity, I was hesitant to test my body's limits. I resorted to eating small, frequent meals throughout the day to avoid stretching my stomach and causing pain. Meanwhile, another five pounds disappeared.

My friends were starting to wonder about me. "You look thin," they would say whenever we'd meet up or run into each other on campus. "Have you been losing weight?"

"I've been sick," I would reply with a sad smile.

"Oh," they would say, and then quickly change the subject. Nobody wanted to talk about being sick. Not even Raleigh wanted to talk about me being sick. There was only so much hashing and rehashing of health issues that a person could handle. I was alone in my unidentifiable illness.

As much as I wanted answers to my medical questions, I was tired of seeing doctors. All they could do was run inconclusive tests and play guessing games. Meanwhile, I was racking up the co-pays and prescription costs. My condition was certainly uncomfortable, and at times excruciating, but it didn't appear to be life-threatening. The most I could do was ignore it, or at least tolerate it. I was done with doctors for the time being.

Chapter 4

"Are we almost there?" Raleigh whined, shaking out his legs in discomfort. We had parked at a rest stop for our second break in less than an hour. We were getting close to our final destination, and would probably get there even sooner if we didn't stop so frequently, but the uncomfortable drive was taking its toll on our bodies. We were getting anxious, and tired.

The air was still surprisingly cool for summer, but with the high elevation, the sun was bright and almost singed our skin as we stood outside. "Almost," I replied, flinching from the sun. "Let's keep moving."

The lonely road soon transitioned into a bustling highway as we approached the cluster of small cities surrounding Denver. We had finally reached the metropolis. Signs denoting the distance to our particular exit assured us we were drawing near to our destination. We were almost home.

"This is it," I said to Raleigh over the walkie-talkie. Only a few more miles and our long journey would finally be at an end. "We're almost there!" Raleigh cheered on the other end.

Following the faithful map, we exited the freeway and beheld a long stretch of road lined with familiar franchises and lesser-known privately owned establishments. The neighborhood looked promising. Clean streets, plenty of shopping, and not a chain-link fence or forsaken building in sight. Not at all the run-down ruins I had envisioned. My excitement grew as a wave of relief washed over me. Things weren't so bad.

Unfortunately, I had let down my guard too soon. My heart sank into the pit of my scarcely recovered stomach as we turned onto the cross street. Tucked behind a questionable-looking convenience store was the minimally maintained apartment complex.

My walkie-talkie crackled. "Is that it?" Raleigh asked skeptically. I had hoped not, but the barely legible, half-missing sign in front of the parking lot said otherwise.

"That's it," I said sadly. "Welcome home."

The place probably had potential early in its existence, but as it stood now, it had failed to reach it. Slightly reminiscent of log cabins, the apartments weren't exactly in shambles, but the number of dingy rugs and dirty towels flung over the patio railings adversely affected the aesthetic. Trash littered the minimal landscaping and several groups of small children ran about the parking lot unattended. A surly group of tank-top-clad men smoking cigarettes eyed me as I pulled into an empty spot.

I knew my doors were locked. I never drove anywhere without ensuring that they were, but I clicked the button anyway for additional reassurance. The familiar snap of the locking mechanism was the only comfort I had in the midst of my strange surroundings. "Raleigh, I'm scared," I whispered into the walkie-talkie.

"You'll be fine," he assured me. "I'll be right there." I waited several minutes as he attempted to maneuver the fourteen-foot beast of a moving truck in the tightly packed parking lot. I saw the group of men throw back their heads in laughter as they watched the scene. I slid down in my seat, as if hiding would protect me from the disconcerting knowledge that this was the environment in which I would be spending the next few years.

Raleigh jumped down from the cabin once he had successfully

parked, and walked over to my window. He tapped the glass, knowing the window hadn't worked in months and I would need to open the door to talk to him.

"Are you okay?" he asked.

"No!" I cried through the minimal crack of the door. I didn't want to open it any more than I absolutely had to, not with strangers milling about. "This place is a dump!"

"It's not that bad," he replied, looking around and only grimacing slightly. He was much more optimistic than I was in my panicked state. "Maybe the insides are really nice."

"I don't care about the insides!" I wailed. "This place is a mess! I don't want to live here!" Tears welled up in my eyes as devastating scenes of being shot or kidnapped, or worse, flashed through my mind.

"Well, what do you want to do?" he asked. We had already paid several hundred dollars in application fees and deposits, none of which was refundable. But even if I could have borne the loss of that cost, we were strangers to the city. We had our entire lives packed in the truck, and with nowhere else to go, we were stuck.

"We don't really have a choice," I replied, reluctantly wiping away the tears. I couldn't bear to think that all my plans had failed and we had made an irrevocable mistake.

Raleigh motioned me out of the car. I glanced around to make sure I was safe from any hoodlums, and slowly got out of the car. He rubbed his hands on my shoulders to comfort me. "It'll be okay," he said, looking into my crying eyes. "If it really sucks, then we'll only have to stay here for a year."

A fresh wave of tears rolled over me. Hadn't I already endured enough packing, enough moving, enough stress? I didn't want to have to move again for three or four years. "I don't want to do this again!" I sobbed. I was already so fragile. I didn't know how much more stress I could take before I completely snapped.

Raleigh pulled me close and let me cry on his shoulder until I calmed down. It took some time, but eventually, my tears subsided. Raleigh pulled away and read my somber expression for any signs of an additional outburst or overreaction. When it appeared that all that remained were the residual, harmless traces of my heightened emotions, he eased out of the caress. I had pulled myself together for the time being.

He made sure the cats were comfortable in the car (or as comfortable as they could be in an unfamiliar place), and we walked through the complex to the main office. With my accordion folder in one hand, I clutched Raleigh's hand with the other. Holding hands wasn't necessarily for protection, but for my own peace of mind that I wasn't going through this frightening situation alone. Along the way, we passed open windows blaring obnoxious music, overtired mothers absentmindedly tending to their many children, and several sets of dumpsters overrun with abandoned property. I shuddered with each sight and tried my best to keep from crying again.

The complex was much larger than I had anticipated, and we walked around in circles before spotting the corner of a pool in the distance. "That must be the main office," I said, and we headed in that direction.

"I'll let you talk to them," Raleigh whispered as he opened the front door. Not that I had much of a choice. With me having done all the planning and arrangements, he didn't know the first thing about the rental application. I'd have to deal with the process all by myself.

We entered the lobby and were greeted by a short, rotund man with gray hair and a beard. "Hi, may I help you?" he asked, barely glancing away from his computer screen.

"We're the Starbucks," I replied. "I've been speaking with Laura about renting an apartment here."

"Laura's out to lunch," he said briskly, still not giving us his full attention. "My name is Vince. May I help you?"

I frowned. All my dealings had been with Laura and I wanted to keep it that way. I didn't like strangers, and I didn't like change. She was my one contact in this unfamiliar place, my one constant throughout the entire renting process. Settling for someone new would have been disruptive to my need for stability. "Do you know when she'll be back?"

"Well, she left a little while ago. It could be another half hour or so if you want to wait." Vince tilted his head in the direction of the two armchairs against the back wall. I glanced behind me. They appeared to be comfortable enough, but I didn't come all that way to sit around.

"I don't, really," I replied tersely. "We've driven sixteen hours from Arizona."

"That's a pretty long drive," he remarked, understanding my reluctance to sit and wait. "Well, what is it you need to do?"

"I've already completed the application," I replied. I pulled out the stack of relevant papers from their section in my accordion folder. "I've also paid the application fee and the deposit." I flipped to the page with the printed confirmation numbers from the electronic transactions, in case he wanted proof.

"So, you only need to sign the lease?" he asked, without as much as a glimpse at the papers in my hand.

"Well, I was hoping we could take a look at the unit first." After all, it was bad enough I had packed up all my belongings and driven sixteen hours to a city I'd never seen before. I wasn't about to sign my life away without at least seeing the apartment in person. Sure, I had already paid the nonrefundable deposit and application fee, but with the lease unsigned, there was still time to back out if the inside of the apartment was absolutely atrocious.

"Oh," Vince said with a frown. He obviously wanted to help me as much as I wanted to be helped by him. He tapped his fingers on the desk and glanced at the clock. He looked at his screen, and then back at me. "Well, I guess we can do the walkthrough until Laura gets back," he finally said.

"Okay," I replied. At least something was getting done.

Vince grabbed some papers from a filing cabinet, ushered us out of the office, and locked the door behind him. He must have been the only employee in the office. Otherwise, he would have left it unlocked. I'm sure he was flustered with having his workflow interrupted, but I was not about to wait around after driving such a long way. In the current situation, I was a prospective client, which meant I took priority over anything else.

We passed by the same disconcerting sights we had seen before, on our walk over to the office. The disheveled state of the complex didn't seem to faze him. How he could rent out such apartments with a clear conscience, I would never know.

Vince broke the silence with a remark about the weather. "I'm sorry it's so hot out!" He glanced back at me as he continued weaving along through a group of young children running haphazardly on the sidewalk.

I almost laughed. It couldn't have been more than eighty degrees outside. That was practically cold, by Arizona standards. That man didn't know the first thing about hot weather. "Are you kidding? It was over a hundred degrees when we left Tucson!"

"A hundred degrees?" he exclaimed. With the way he responded, I might as well have been living on the sun. That was an obscene temperature for someone who was used to mild weather. "It's been an unusually hot summer, but nowhere near *that* hot."

"How are the winters?" I asked. I already had an idea based on my internet-based research, but I was curious to hear from a Colorado native.

"The winters are usually pretty mild. Sometimes it snows several inches, but it hardly ever sticks for more than a day or two."

I scrunched my nose. The most contact I had ever had with snow was during a brief visit to the mountains when I was still living in California as a child. Since then, I'd grown accustomed to warm weather and actually abhorred the cold. But Raleigh, as I could tell from the smile flickering across his face, was excited about having a white winter for a change. Coming from Arizona, land of the blazing sun, I could only imagine that I would be miserable having to acclimate to such an extreme.

"Well, this is it," Vince announced. We were facing a second-story unit at the back of the complex. Not a long walk by athletic standards, but enough to tire me out since Raleigh and I had already gotten lost in the large complex beforehand. I caught my breath while the leasing agent fumbled with his keys. When he finally unlocked the door, I gasped.

There, covering the entire length of the high ceiling, were the exposed beams I had always dreamed about. They were a few shades lighter than the ones I had been admiring at the convenience store earlier that day, but nonetheless spectacular. Surely, then, it was destiny that everything was going to be okay. We were meant to live there in that dingy apartment.

But destiny or not, that didn't stop me from scrutinizing every inch of the interior as we conducted the walkthrough. I made sure to point out every speck on the carpet and every imperfection in the paint. I even noted the gaps between the wall and some of the electrical outlets—damage that was not even listed on the form and had to be handwritten on the side. The agent's ballpoint pen scribbled furiously as he struggled to keep up with my endless string of remarks and criticisms.

Based on the collective sigh, both Vince and Raleigh were relieved when I had completed my thorough examination of the apartment. But I had to ensure that my analysis was complete. I didn't want any previous damage to be attributed to Raleigh and me when we vacated the unit. The agent locked up and led us back through the maze to the main office.

By that time, Laura had returned from her lunch. Vince quickly pawned us off on her and returned to his tasks. She forced a smile on her otherwise somber face and sat us down with a thick stack of papers. She attempted polite yet unobtrusive conversation as I scanned each line of the lease for any questionable clauses. She seemed tired, but I was tired too. On some level, we connected with each other in our mutual misery.

After we had finished signing all the papers and paying the prorated portion of our first month's rent, she handed us the keys to the unit and a map of the complex. "Welcome to our community," she said flatly. On our way out of the office, an unattended child nearly ran me over while speeding down the sidewalk on his bicycle.

Some community.

"Well, we're finally here," Raleigh said as we retrieved the cats from the car. We had somewhat of an idea of where we were going, especially now that we had a map, so we navigated through the complex with much more confidence. "What are we going to do now?" he asked.

"I need to eat first before I can do anything," I said sharply. My hunger pains were ravaging my stomach, and with the amount of work that remained, I knew my irritability would make a monster out of me if I didn't eat something soon.

"Then what?" he asked, shifting the pet carrier from one hand to the other. His whole body leaned over in that direction and his speed slowed as he struggled with the weight. "I thought maybe we could relax."

"Relax?" I cried, shifting the crate I had in my own hand over to the other. How could I possibly relax when there were so many things I needed to do? "We don't have time to relax. We've got too much work to do."

"Work? What work?" He thought the hard part was done now that we had finally reached our destination, but since I had done all the planning pertaining to our relocation, he was oblivious to all the move-related tasks that still loomed over us. And, with me starting work in one week, we would have to work fast to get everything done in time. Taking a break would have been foolish.

"Well, we've got to start unpacking the truck, for starters."

"But honey, that's what the movers are for," he reminded me. True—there was a team of two men coming to unload the truck in the morning. We had endured enough unpleasantness with two moves in one summer, both under the scorching sun. My patience was even more limited than my stamina, so we had opted to hire movers for this final round.

Even so, that wasn't good enough for me. I needed to get things started. "Yeah, I know," I said, "but the voucher for the movers is only valid for two hours. Anything beyond that costs extra."

Raleigh seemed confused and continued to argue with me. "It's a one-bedroom apartment. I seriously doubt it'll take longer than two hours for them to get the stuff upstairs."

"You don't understand!" I shrieked. "They start the clock as soon as they depart from their facility. It's half an hour away, which means they'll only have an hour and a half to unload the truck."

Raleigh contemplated these facts for a moment, and then whined, "I really don't want to do any more moving! Can we *please* leave it to the movers? It's not going to take longer than an hour and a half!"

"I'm not taking any chances," I said firmly as I walked up the stairs to our unit. My money was at stake, and I was not about to part ways with it so easily. "We need to get started tonight." The case was closed, but that didn't stop Raleigh from expressing his frustration and disapproval with a pronounced frown.

With the cats tucked away and terrified in their new home, we departed for our long-awaited dinner. We had originally planned to eat at a local Chinese restaurant, for which I had purchased a voucher to maximize the amount of food we could get for the money. And, of course, I had already printed out a detailed set of directions from the apartment to the restaurant. After all, a strange city called for desperate measures.

As we waited to turn at a street light, I spotted a familiar logo in the shopping center across the way. I thought I had seen the name before, but I couldn't quite pinpoint where. Then I realized why the place looked so familiar. "I think I have a voucher for that place, too," I said.

"What?" Raleigh asked, looking around. There was an open field to our left, and a twenty-story medical complex to our right. He didn't see the quaint little Mexican restaurant tucked away in the shopping center diagonally across from us.

I pointed to the restaurant. The pink stucco stood out against the neutral façades of the surrounding buildings. Boldly colored cursive font proudly displayed the restaurant's name on the side. "In fact, I *know* I have a voucher for that place."

"How many vouchers did you buy?" he asked, surprised. He seemed offended that I hadn't consulted him regarding the purchases and financial decisions I had been making involving the move. Since I had taken it upon myself to conduct all the research and planning, I figured I had earned the right to make executive decisions. That being the case, I started scouting the Denver deals weeks before we even moved out there, just to be sure I wouldn't miss anything good. In my fervor, I had purchased quite a few vouchers for nearby establishments. After all, we were on a limited budget, and with our things inaccessible until we unpacked and settled in, I knew we were going to have to go out to eat for the first few days. Stocking up on vouchers was the only smart way to go about it.

"Don't worry about it," I said quickly, redirecting the conversation. "Would you rather eat there, or would you rather stick to the original plan?"

"I don't know. What is it?"

"It's Mexican," I replied. "Would you rather have Mexican or Chinese?"

"I don't know," he sighed with annoyance. "You're driving, you decide!"

"Hurry up, the light's going to change!" I screeched. "What would you rather have?"

"Mexican, I guess!" he shouted as I made my turn.

Mexican it was then.

As I pulled into the parking lot, I saw that most of the restaurant's spaces were empty. My skin crawled with anxiety, as an empty parking lot was usually a bad sign. Once inside, we were lukewarmly greeted by a barely pubescent boy who showed us to our table. The interior of the restaurant, like its exterior counterpart, was vacant. Only one other couple occupied the massive dining floor. Again, not a good sign.

The waiter who tended to us was friendly, but he hardly spoke a word of English. I asked Raleigh to order for me in Spanish to ensure that my meal would be prepared according to my liking. In my ravenous state of hunger, the last thing I wanted was to have to send back my food due to a miscommunication.

Ordering, of course, only took place after I had intensely studied the menu and weighed the cost of each entrée against the calorie content to find a reasonable middle ground. Raleigh, who had given up on trying to argue with me as I debated with myself, crossed his arms and waited for me make up my mind. His sighs only ceased when the waiter brought a basket of chips and salsa to distract him.

The meal itself was bland. I quickly understood why the parking lot and restaurant had been so empty. Even so, the substantiality of it was appreciated. We had endured a long day, and there was a daunting task ahead of us. After dousing the food with a flood of lemon juice, I forced a reasonable amount down my throat. I consoled myself with the knowledge that spinach and seafood stuffed enchiladas weren't entirely unhealthy, and felt satisfied.

The portions were generous, so I asked for a to-go box for the second half of my meal. Raleigh, who had quickly consumed his entire combination platter along with a whole basket of tortilla chips, scolded me for not eating any of the chips, but I had learned my lesson earlier that day. And besides, eating half the entrée was daring enough. No need to add extra calories on top of that.

We left a tip for the waiter and headed back to the apartment to tackle the task of unloading the truck. On our way there, I spotted a sign beside the road welcoming us to the city of Denver, elevation 5,280 feet. We must have crossed into an adjoining city on our quest for dinner. I wouldn't have even noticed had it not been for the sign. Tucson was a big city with little in the way of surrounding suburbs. We never had to leave town, and even if we had wanted to, it would have required an hour-long drive to the next municipality. Now, being so close to surrounding neighborhoods without the long trek was a refreshing change.

With our hunger satiated, we got to work. "How much of this stuff do we have to take up?" Raleigh asked, his arms straining with an oversized carton containing our entire collection of pots and pans.

"As much as we can," I replied, struggling even with the much smaller load of kitchen gadgets. "I'm not taking any chances with those movers in the morning."

We painstakingly transported about a fourth of our possessions from the truck, our strength waning with each successive box. I wanted to get at least the essentials, such as the toiletries and cooking supplies, unloaded immediately because we would need to use those items right away. Finally, when even walking down the stairs proved to be too physically demanding for me, I relinquished my efforts.

"I guess that'll have to do," I sighed.

We hadn't unloaded any of the furniture, so the two of us settled onto the bare carpet for a break. Our two cats cowered in the corner of the living room, terrified of the wide-open and unfamiliar space. They didn't have anywhere to hide.

"I hate to bring this up," Raleigh started, "but we don't have any food in the house. We'll have to go to the store and pick up a few things." He was right. We had consumed the remainder of our perishables before we left Tucson, and what we didn't eat, we left in the fridge for the enjoyment of the owner of the house once she returned. We didn't even have a can of soup to our name.

"Tonight?" I asked. My whole body ached from sitting in the

car for eight hours and hauling boxes up the stairs for another two. I didn't want to move another inch.

"Well, you're going to want to eat breakfast in the morning, aren't you?" Of course, I would want to eat breakfast in the morning. And second breakfast, and lunch, and dinner, and supper, and who knew what else. Eating, even with all my caloric limitations and particular requests, had become essential to the maintenance of my mood. I was unhappy when I was hungry. And with all the unpacking we would have to do, I was going to need my strength, and lots of it, too.

Even so, I groaned. The workload never seemed to let up.

We cut our break short and ventured out to the nearest grocery store, which, thankfully, was only across the street. For the first time in my life, I hadn't planned a menu or made a list. We grabbed whatever looked good, making sure we had enough quick and easy meals to get us through the next few days. The spontaneity of unplanned purchases and impulse buys was atypical for me, but I almost enjoyed it.

By the time we exited the store, the moderately cool Colorado air had turned into a brisk chill. Still dressed in shorts and T-shirts, we shivered as we crossed the parking lot to our car. We weren't expecting the temperature to drop so rapidly. The shifting weather would require a hearty dose of adjustment.

With the groceries put away and our long day drawing to a close, we threw down some pillows and spread out the few blankets we owned onto the carpet as a makeshift bed. The hard floor was uncomfortable, but there was solace in knowing we had at least reached the first benchmark in our adventure. After months of wondering where we were going to live, and weeks of planning how we were going to get there, we had finally arrived. It wasn't quite what we were expecting, but it was home.

Chapter 5

THE NEXT MORNING I AWOKE TO THE BEAUTIFUL SIGHT OF THE exposed beams on the ceiling. The interior of the apartment was entirely bare, but the rustic charm of the ceiling made the place feel like home. Having that one small dream fulfilled gave me the energy and encouragement I needed to start my day. Despite the searing pain ripping my spine from having slept on the living room floor, I smiled and sighed with the satisfaction of knowing that Raleigh and I would soon be completely settled into our new home. It would take some time, and probably an extra dose of patience on my part, but we would get through the process well enough.

The movers called, right on schedule, to inform me they were departing their facility. Raleigh and I ate a quick and effortless breakfast of cereal as we waited for them to arrive. When half an hour had passed and the movers still hadn't arrived, I became concerned. The clock was ticking on my dime. I fidgeted in frustration. I loathed standing around, waiting, but there wasn't much I could do while most of my belongings were still packed away in the truck. I had no choice but to pace the living room and attempt not to let my annoyance seize control of my senses.

Raleigh took the opportunity to retrieve the moving truck, which he had parked on the far side of the lot so it would be out of the way. After much maneuvering around the tight turns of the parking lot, he pulled the truck up to the curb closest to our building for easy access. The farther the movers had to walk to our unit, the more time it would take them to unload the truck. We were prepared for their arrival, even if there still wasn't any sign of them.

Finally, my phone rang and the number that had called earlier that morning to inform me of the dispatch flashed across the screen. The man on the other line apologized for the delay and reported that he and his associate had finally arrived. I was relieved, too, because it was still early in the day and my limited supply of patience was already running out.

Having spent the past forty-five minutes milling about the empty living room unproductively, I walked out to the parking lot to meet the two-man crew. The person I had been speaking to on the phone, a young man with dusty blonde hair and a lean, muscular build, stepped out of the truck and apologized profusely for the inconvenience. He said they had forgotten some equipment at the main office, and while en route, realized his error and had to turn back to retrieve it. That error, combined with the considerable amount of morning rush-hour traffic, had resulted in their arriving fifteen minutes past their anticipated time. I expressed my monetary concern to the young man, since it was not my fault they were behind schedule. He kindly said he would credit me the excess fifteen minutes, for which I was grateful.

I quickly realized the fifteen-minute credit was entirely unnecessary. The two men carried two or three boxes at a time up the flight of stairs without so much as a heavy sigh or drop of sweat. It was impressive—neither Raleigh nor I had previously witnessed such unyielding strength. After all, we had tuckered out after carrying up only a few boxes the night before! It didn't

STRESS SIZE

take the two men longer than half an hour to unload the moving truck, living room furniture and all.

I was relieved at the expediency but also annoyed that I had made such a big deal about getting a head start the night before. All that work had been completely unnecessary. Raleigh raised his eyebrows at me upon realizing this, but thankfully, refrained from rubbing the incident in my face. We tipped the movers and dove into the immense task of unpacking our belongings.

Initially, I had wanted to start my new job right away. Wasting time—even a week—would mean the loss of several hundred dollars. But company policy stated I could only start my new position at the beginning of a pay period. This meant I had a whole week off to unpack and settle into the apartment. As I stood among a half a dozen open boxes, knee-deep in crumpled newspapers, I was grateful for the extra time. Starting a new job was going to be stressful enough, but attempting to do so without even having unpacked would have been impossible.

Unpacking the contents of our one-bedroom abode only took so long, especially without a dresser and bedside tables in which to store our clothes and bedside belongings. Raleigh and I had spent the last two years utilizing a loaner set that belonged to our previous apartment complex, so apart from the queen-sized mattress and box spring, we didn't actually own any bedroom furniture. And since that apartment had been so small we didn't have a dining room set either. Our new, oversized one-bedroom unit seemed empty with only the sofa and end tables to fill it.

Raleigh and I took advantage of the remainder of the week at our disposal by hunting down some adequate furniture to fill the vacant dining room and bedroom. I had started my furniture search weeks before we even arrived, and while we still had possession of the moving truck, we made arrangements to pick up the beautiful inlaid seven-piece dining set I had discovered in an online advertisement. We also shopped around for a bedroom set, which, only after driving all over town and stopping at nearly a dozen stores to satisfy my compulsive desire to comparison shop, we eventually ordered from the first store we had visited.

I wasn't thrilled about spending so much money upfront, but Raleigh managed to convince me it was for the best. After all, a cardboard box containing a haphazard pile of socks could only be so efficient. He reminded me that with the upcoming stresses of working a full-time job, let alone one on a rotating shift, I would want as much convenience and organization as possible. As usual, he was right. With the additional furniture moved in and the last of our boxes unpacked, the dingy apartment started to feel like the cozy home I had always envisioned.

When we weren't unpacking, hanging up pictures, or trying to decide which furniture finish would be best suited to our new abode, we drove around to see the sights. We came across several meticulously maintained, sprawling parks—a few of the over two hundred scattered about the city. We also browsed through a handful of thrift stores and antique malls to get decorating ideas for our new place. And, thanks to one of my trusty vouchers, we also discovered a delightful little tea shop that served the most delicious freshly steeped loose leaf tea and flaky, buttery scones with Devonshire cream and fruit preserves. We had only been Denver residents for a week, but we were quickly settling in.

Even though familiarizing ourselves with the city made the strange place feel more like home, our life was lacking. It had been months since we had graduated from school, and even longer since we had spent quality time with our friends. We needed contact and conversation. We needed to get out and meet some new people. This would be difficult to do since we had moved to town without so much as an acquaintance. With most of the unpacking and settling in finally accomplished, I suggested to Raleigh that we try going to church.

"Church?" Raleigh asked skeptically. "Neither of us has been to church in years." That was true. In fact, the last time either of us had set foot in a church was the day we had gotten married, nearly two and a half years before. It had been even longer since we had sat down for service. Somehow, between going to school, working part-time, and adjusting to our newly joined lives, our tightly packed schedules couldn't squeeze in weekly sermons. My spirituality seemed to slip by the wayside.

"That doesn't mean we can't start going now," I responded. "How else are we going to meet new people?" We were still young, but we were a quiet, married couple. We weren't exactly the type of folks that went out on the town, bar hopping and dancing and whatnot. We enjoyed the finer things in life—fine dining, foreign films, and intellectually stimulating conversation. From what we had encountered in college, not many people our age could see beyond the glare of their smartphones and other gadgets and gizmos to truly appreciate those activities. We were alone in our interests.

"Aren't you going to meet people at work?" Raleigh asked. He seemed reluctant to venture back into a chapel, even if it meant finally getting to meet some new people. He sat on the couch, a nearly motionless mass, entirely unenthused.

"Yeah, my associates," I replied, rolling my eyes. He obviously didn't understand the delicate dynamics of the workplace. "But I'll be an assistant manager. I can't exactly hang out with them outside of work. That would be inappropriate, a conflict of interest or something."

"Well, what about the other managers? Can't you hang out

with *them*?" he suggested, still avoiding my initial solution to our solitary situation.

Raleigh's lack of experience as an employee was exceedingly apparent. People who worked together didn't hang out together outside of work. That wasn't the way things happened. After spending so much time together each day, encountering a different set of people was refreshing, if not required, for the preservation of sanity. "First of all, they'll probably be way older than me," I replied. "We might not have the same interests. Second of all, we might not get along well enough to warrant spending time together outside of our usual shifts. And think about it—if *I'm* not there at the store, then they will be. Somebody's got to be there."

"I see," Raleigh replied flatly. His interest in the subject was waning. He didn't seem to care at all if we spent the rest of our lives cooped up in our apartment without so much as an acquaintance to fall back on.

"Do you not want to go to church?" I asked.

Raleigh thought for a moment, his eyes narrowing with the most consideration he had exhibited since I initiated the conversation. "No, it's not that," he replied. "I wouldn't mind going to church. It's that ... I'm concerned."

"Concerned?" I asked, surprised. With his face having remained blank for much of our discussion, he hadn't appeared to be worried at all. "Concerned about what?"

"Are you even going to have time for that?" he wondered.

I pondered his question. I knew I would be working full-time, and even overtime, according to the job offer letter I had received from the human resources director. And, with the rotating shifts and different schedules each week, my availability would be extremely limited. At the most, I'd only be able to make it to half of the services in a given month—and that was the best-case

STRESS SIZE

scenario. The actual results might even be less. As an assistant store manager whose very job description dictated wide-open scheduling availability with no caveats, I couldn't walk into work and insist on having Sundays off. That wasn't possible. But I didn't want something like a stressful job to make my life lonely and miserable. I wanted to at least *try* going to church. If the trek to the chapel proved too stressful for my tight schedule, I could live with the satisfaction of knowing I had at least attempted to revive my social life.

"I've never had time before," I finally answered. "What difference does that make?"

"You haven't even started working yet. Aren't you going to be working a rotating schedule or something?"

"Yeah, so?"

"So, maybe it's too soon for you to be venturing out and trying to make new friends and stuff. You should probably rest up while you still have the chance. Once you start working, you're going to be really stressed. I don't think you should try and take on anything else."

"But I can't sit here by myself," I said sadly. Only one week in, and I was already feeling the isolation of being a stranger to a new city. I would wither away if I had to endure life without any friends.

"You're not by yourself, you have me," he observed, offended by my remark.

"Yeah, but..." What should have been a simple suggestion was turning into a complicated conversation. I wasn't sure I wanted to delve that deep, especially not into the dynamics of our relationship.

"But what?" Raleigh demanded. "Am I not enough?"

"Raleigh," I sighed. It appeared that this discussion, however painful or uncomfortable, was necessary. I proceeded, with caution. "It's not healthy for us to sit here by ourselves. I'll at least see people at work, but what are *you* going to do? How are you going to be social by sitting at home all day?" I asked with as much concern for his isolation as I could muster in my own solitary state. Raleigh had been postponing his job search, so he was unemployed for the foreseeable future. He wouldn't exactly be getting out much, and that worried me.

"I guess you're right," he admitted reluctantly. He must have realized that without a job to go to every day, he would be deprived of interaction with anyone other than me. "Well, then," he replied. "I guess we'll try going to church!"

I sighed, relieved that he had finally come to his senses. That night I conducted an internet search for "cool, hip churches." I had suffered through enough long-winded and outdated sermons as a child and wanted to be around like-minded people my own age. My search revealed a couple of congregations whose interests and beliefs appeared to correspond with our own. I even listened to a few snippets of the previous sermons to see if I liked the pastors. I looked up the service hours, location, and directions to my top pick.

What I hadn't looked up was an alternate route. Being so new to the area, I couldn't have anticipated there would be a biking marathon running right through my intended path. We had left the house early to allow for any wrong turns, but as we ventured into downtown Denver, every other street seemed to be closed off for the race. With a multitude of one-way streets, turn only lanes, roundabouts, and dead ends, we quickly became lost.

To make matters worse, the traffic was backed up bumper to bumper. We were trapped in the gridlock alongside the skyscrapers. There was no way we were going to make it to the service on time. "This wasn't how it was supposed to happen!" I shouted, tears rolling down my face. I shook the steering wheel in frustration.

"Maybe it's a sign that it's too soon," Raleigh suggested.

"But how else am I supposed to make new friends?" I cried. In my frustration, I couldn't see any other way of making connections. "We *have* to go to church!" I declared resolutely. Just then, we inched by a large cathedral whose congregation appeared to be trickling in. "We could go there," I suggested desperately. "They haven't even started yet."

"Where are you going to park?" Raleigh pointed out. The tightly packed cars made changing lanes, let alone finding a parking spot in a meter-based system, nearly impossible.

"Ugh!" I shouted, rattling the steering wheel again as we passed by the cathedral with its spires scratching the sky.

By the time we made it through the detour, we were already half an hour late, and we didn't even know where we were. Based on the heights of the buildings, it looked like we were exiting downtown, but I had only printed out directions to the church. I didn't have a detailed street map. There was no way I would be able to find the building. And besides, even if I had gotten my bearings, we would have been unpardonably late to the service. We couldn't barge in smack in the middle of the sermon. Sadly, our quest would have to be cast aside.

Chapter 6

Between unpacking, furniture shopping, exploring the neighborhood, and getting lost, my first day of work quickly approached. I was excited to start working (even more so to start earning more money), but I was not thrilled about the drive. My "home store," as Alisha, the human resources director, had described it, would be much closer to my apartment. But I wouldn't get to start working at that location until after I completed my training. The six weeks of training would take place at a store nearly forty-five minutes away from where I lived. The training was mandatory, and the location of the training store was not my decision. My fate was in the hands of the human resources director.

Inconvenience aside, I was grateful the training wasn't taking place at the store located downtown. A long drive I could handle, but having to deal with the dangers of downtown would have terrified me. I had already had my brief yet unpleasant encounter with navigating the complex maze of one-way avenues and dead-end cross streets during my failed attempt to find the church. I didn't want to have to deal with the crime and poverty too, especially when getting off late at night or arriving early in the morning. Anything could happen to a young woman in a dark and unfamiliar part of town.

On the morning of my first day, I left the house an hour before

STRESS SIZE

I was scheduled to arrive at the store. Much to my dismay, I barely arrived on time after sitting in snail's-pace rush-hour traffic. Thankfully, the directions were fairly straightforward and I didn't have any issues finding the place. It was pretty much a straight shot on the freeway, twenty exits north.

An energetic man with short, black hair unlocked the front door of the building as I approached. He glanced at my name tag, which I had already clipped to my shirt in preparation for the workday, and upon recognizing my name, greeted me warmly.

"Hi, Nicole. Nice to meet you," he said, shaking my hand vigorously. "I'm Jeff. I'm the store manager for this location and I'll be overseeing your training for the next six weeks."

He walked briskly through the store, which had not yet opened for business for the day. He paused briefly now and then to proudly show off the various departments and displays. Apart from being slightly more organized, the store looked like all others in the massive retail chain. But he had obviously invested a lot of time and energy into his store's layout and presentation and wanted to share it with someone fresh and impressionable.

Although the store was still closed and most of the employees had not yet arrived, he showed me to the stockroom and introduced me to the members of the stock team. I immediately noticed the earbuds stretching out from underneath their blue shirts, as well as each of the associates' missing name tags. Both offenses were strictly against company policy. In my effort to follow the rules by the book, I didn't hesitate in pointing out these errors.

"Where is your name tag?" I asked one of the girls as Jeff introduced us. I pointed to my own white badge, engraved with my name in bold blue letters. It was a gift from the company for having completed my first year of service. At the very least, the girl should have been wearing the standard-issue, sticker label alternative.

She looked down at her shirt and shrugged. "I don't know. I never wear my name tag."

For a brief moment, the grin on Jeff's face disappeared. Embarrassed that I had caught a flaw in the appearance of his staff, he said to her sternly, "You should always wear your name tag. It's company policy."

"But I'm on the stock team!" she argued, waving around the plastic-covered merchandise she had in hand for emphasis. "Most of the time I'm gone before the customers even get here!"

"Just make sure you wear it from now on," he warned. With his smile having returned, he turned to me and said, "Great attention to detail. You're going to do great here!"

I smiled back, proud of myself for not only adhering to company policy but for urging others to do the same. The girl shot me a dirty look as Jeff and I left the stockroom. She clearly didn't share my respect for the rules.

When we finally arrived at the break room adjoining the office, Jeff allowed me a brief opportunity to set down my belongings. I stuck my sack lunch in the fridge and stowed my purse in one of the empty lockers. Jeff then plopped me down into an oversized rolling chair in the office with a three-inch thick three-ringed binder bursting with booklets. The binder landed with a resounded thud as he tossed it onto the desk in front of me.

"What's this?" I asked. My eyes widened at the four or five hundred pages stacked in front of me in an ominous pile.

"That," he replied with a big grin, "is all of your training modules."

"Modules, as in plural?" I asked, flipping through the hundreds of pages of written material outlining training objectives, management techniques, and business strategies. There were charts, diagrams, and spreadsheets. Formulas, statistics, and calculations I couldn't even begin to comprehend. It was much more information about the inside and outside of the company than I ever cared to learn. I was overwhelmed.

"Modules, plural, as in twenty-five of them. Six whole weeks' worth of reading!" he replied enthusiastically. He flipped to a particular page in the binder and pointed at a day-by-day outline. "See? Each day of training has its own set of modules and corresponding tasks. It even breaks it down by the allotted number of hours for any given activity. It's a combination of in-depth reading with on-the-job training. Pretty neat, huh?" I didn't think it was possible, but his smile got even wider. He seemed to be genuinely excited about the material he would be teaching me over the next several weeks.

I, on the other hand, was not so enthused. I resisted the urge to frown as I feigned enthusiasm. "Yeah, so organized!" I replied with a forced smile.

The heap of dry material set out on the desk presented a seemingly impossible amount of reading. Six weeks wasn't a long time for such a daunting task, especially when the reading was to be accompanied by activities and on-the-job training. There was no way I was going to get through all of it, at least not without skimming some of the pages or skipping some of the activities. The thought of cutting corners irked me. I had always been an overachiever, the type of person that gave at least 100 percent in any given situation.

The task simply couldn't be avoided. I knew I had to get started right away if I had any chance of finishing without taking shortcuts. I glanced down at the pages in front of me and saw there was another training calendar that squeezed the curriculum into three weeks. "What's that?" I asked Jeff, pointing to the page. Six weeks was going to be short enough—three weeks would be impossibly brief.

"Oh, that?" he waved his hand through the air, as if to dismiss the calendar. "That's for the regularly recruited managers, the ones that get promoted from area supervisor or come into the job from outside the company. They only get three weeks of training. But don't worry—you're a college recruit. You're special. You get an extra three weeks to take your time," he beamed.

When only moments ago I had been bemoaning the mere six weeks of training, I now found myself incredibly grateful. I had been with the company for two years and was fairly familiar with all the standards and procedures at the associate level. That hands-on knowledge would give me a definite advantage as I went deeper into the company's practices from a managerial standpoint. I couldn't imagine being recently promoted, or worse, being recruited from outside the company with absolutely no prior knowledge of the company's particular methods, and be expected to do a decent job after three weeks of training. That seemed like too much for a person to handle.

Not wanting to waste time, no matter how much I had graciously been granted, I flipped through the binder and turned my attention toward the first page. I had hardly taken a peek before Jeff whisked me away to another room. My studies would have to be postponed.

The door to the next room was locked, and the room itself very small. The space was uncomfortably intimate for a couple of strangers, let alone retail professionals. For a brief moment, I feared that something terrible might happen to me. But I saw that the room was monitored by a surveillance camera and quickly cast my concerns aside.

STRESS SIZE

Jeff immediately dove into a verbal explanation of various cash-handling procedures and security measures, none of which were familiar to me, having only been a part-time cashier and fitting room attendant. When he noted the confusion on my face, he pulled out a thick stack of papers and started flipping through them as he explained the procedures again, but none of it made any sense without being shown the actual steps in person. My eyes only became wider as I became more confused.

"Maybe we'll try going over it again tomorrow," he said, still smiling wildly, even when faced with my wide-eyed terror. He put the papers away in their appropriate location and led me back to the office.

By that time, the district manager and the district loss prevention manager had arrived at the store. I had been hoping to meet the human resources manager, the woman who had hired me, but I was told that although she had every intention of seeing me off on my first day in my new position, she got caught up at her office and couldn't quite make it out to the store. So I was stuck in the back office, no camera, no windows, with three male strangers. Again I worried something bad might happen to me in that compromising situation.

Sitting in the secluded room with three grown men, I became keenly aware of my age and gender. There was hardly a soul in the store, and anything could have happened without anyone being the wiser. But with their frequent references to vulgar comedies, I realized they weren't much of a threat to me. They were merely a group of immature, overgrown boys. I felt somewhat safer, although it disconcerted me that the fate of the company lay in the hands of men who deeply appreciated bodily humor. I guess that's what I was there for—to slap some sense into the mix.

I felt like an outcast as the three men continued their long spiel of inside jokes, movie quotes, and reinterpretations of slapstick comedy skits. I was relieved when the managers all tried their best to put on a straight face when the first of the sales floor associates arrived for their shift. But every once in a while, they'd elbow each other in the side, let out a snicker or two, or rattle off another meaningless quote from some movie I'd never seen. I fidgeted in my black dress slacks and bright blue blouse, partly because the new shoes I had bought were unbearably uncomfortable, but mostly because I couldn't believe I'd have to spend the day in such an awkward social situation.

Once all the morning employees had put away their belongings and clocked in, Jeff held a rally meeting in the front by the cash registers to inform the associates of the week's objectives. He went over some of the recent sales statistics and reviewed some of the company tenets to bolster morale and get the associates motivated about the minimum wage work they were accomplishing. He made a big deal about introducing me to everyone and welcoming me to the company. Most of them cheered rather flatly, but some of them gleamed at me with sincere grins. I imagined it must have been difficult, in their modest position, to get excited about someone else moving up in the world. They might even have been jealous.

With the rally meeting over, Jeff unlocked the front doors and let the first of the customers inside. As we walked back to the office with the district managers in tow, he explained to me that they were a low-volume store, which had its own scheduling challenges, but pretty much meant I could concentrate on reading my modules for most of the day. Having gotten most of their boyish antics out of their systems, the district managers set up a station in the office in preparation for a lengthy conference call. Jeff got me situated in the adjoining break room with the modules assigned for the day before scurrying off to tend to other tasks in the store.

By that time, several hours had passed since I had eaten breakfast. The emptiness in the pit of my stomach gnawed at my insides. When Jeff popped back in briefly to check on me, I timidly asked about taking a break.

"A break?" he asked, as if the concept was completely foreign to him. He furrowed his eyebrows in confusion. "I guess you can eat a quick snack if you want," he said slowly, discouragingly. "We don't really take breaks as managers. Sometimes, we don't even take lunch."

Pulling a ten-hour shift with no breaks? No lunch? That was crazy—impossible for someone like me who needed to eat at least a little something every other hour or so. My lightning speed metabolism wouldn't have it any other way. But I didn't want to appear weak in front of him, or the other store managers, who I hadn't met yet. Especially not on my first day.

"Oh, I see. Well, I'm fine. I was just wondering," I lied, turning my attention back to some timetable listed on the page.

Really, with the ravenous hunger chewing away at my intestines, I felt like I was dying. With each foodless moment that passed, I found it more and more difficult to concentrate on the subject matter. Whole pages passed before I realized I was skimming over the words without actually reading them. I couldn't get any work done on an empty stomach.

I was very much relieved when, nearly two hours later, Jeff strolled back into the otherwise empty break room and announced he was going to take lunch. Since he was going to be out of the building, I could go ahead and take mine as well. That was gracious of him, but by that time, I had grown so hungry that I knew the small soup I had brought for lunch wouldn't hold me over until the end of the day.

"What's around here to eat for lunch?" I asked, trying not to sound as desperate as the sharp hunger pains in my stomach were making me feel.

"Well, there's a whole bunch of fast food places about a mile down the highway," he said, rattling off a list of less than desirable junk food joints. He even went so far as to provide verbal directions to the restaurant-lined avenue.

Since it was my first time that far north in the metro, none of the exits or streets he described sounded familiar. I was not about to go venturing through town without a map, even during the hour-long lunch with plenty of time to allow for getting lost. "Is there anything in this shopping center?" I asked. The store was situated in a promenade, an outdoor mall with dozens of other shops. Surely there had to be somewhere nearby that would be easy to find and wouldn't massacre my calorie quota.

"Not really," he answered. He then added, "Well, there's an Italian restaurant on the other side of the parking lot. The food's pretty good, but it's kind of pricey." He didn't sound too enthused, not when the prospect of greasy, beef-stuffed tacos enticed him.

At that point, I was so hungry I didn't care if I had to empty out my entire pocketbook to get some quality food. As long as I didn't have to eat a cheeseburger and french fries. "That's fine, thanks," I replied.

We parted ways and I inched across the parking lot in the stiff black shoes that were starting to cut into my ankles. I worried, briefly, about how much my meal would cost, but I reminded myself that it was my first day of work and I deserved a special treat. Even so, that didn't stop me from hesitating when I examined the lunch menu posted outside the restaurant. Ten dollars for a soup, or twelve dollars for a salad—my pick.

I groaned. Eating always seemed to turn into an issue. But the way one of the salads was described on the menu sounded delicious—mixed baby greens gently tossed with golden beets, goat cheese, candied walnuts, and lightly sweetened balsamic vinaigrette. Infinitely better than a cheeseburger and french fries, or any other cheap fast food.

I walked into the restaurant and was surprised to find it completely empty. It was smack in the middle of the prime lunch hour, so I was sure there would be a mad rush. There wasn't. I worried that maybe that meant the food wasn't any good. But I had to realize they were conducting business on the outskirts of town, and they were rather pricey. That limited the clientele quite a bit.

I stood up front for several minutes before the waiter drifting by realized he had been neglecting his hospitality duties. He quickly apologized for the inconvenience and showed me to a table elegantly lined with a crisp white tablecloth. Complete with dark red napkins, fresh flowers, beautifully cut drinking glasses, and coordinating silverware, the setup presented quite an upscale experience.

I ordered the salad I had seen listed outside. The waiter brought me a basket of sliced French bread to whet my appetite. I picked at the pieces slowly, lightly dipping each morsel into the pool of balsamic vinegar swimming with olive oil. Mostly, I wanted the balsamic vinegar, but I found that even with the olive oil the soft, doughy texture of the bread beautifully accompanied the crisp salad that arrived shortly thereafter. I was in fresh food heaven.

When I had finished my meal, I realized I still had nearly half an hour left of my lunch break. I had never been given an hour-long lunch before and hadn't realized how much time sixty minutes really was. Even with my ankles screaming in agony, I took the opportunity to stroll through the promenade. Walking would at least allow me to work off some of the food I had consumed.

I passed by the same sets of stores featured in all the other shopping malls I had ever visited. The repertoire of retailers rarely varied. But the combination of slightly cool air with the bright warm sun made the browsing much more enjoyable, and the fresh air was invigorating after having been cooped up inside the store for the first half of the day. With the number of hours I would be working each day, I wouldn't be getting out much. I needed to take advantage of the fresh air while I could.

During my walk, I came across a kiosk selling gourmet cupcakes. I had always been a sucker for light, fluffy frosting and was tempted by one of the decadent cupcakes the shop had on display. The price per cupcake was exorbitant—more than it would have cost to bake a whole batch myself. When I began walking away from the kiosk empty-handed, the cashier suggested one of the day-old varieties, which were priced at half-off. I simply couldn't resist.

I asked for a knife and fork, with every intention of splitting the cupcake in half and sharing it with Raleigh. After all, the cupcake probably contained the remaining balance of the calories I could reasonably consume for the rest of the day. But when I bit into the soft, sweet crumb topped with thick, creamy frosting, I abandoned my plan. I ate the entire cupcake myself and enjoyed every morsel. Only afterward, when I realized the severity of what I had done, did I feel guilty for not allowing Raleigh the opportunity to indulge in the same confectionary joy.

At any rate, when I returned to the store after my leisurely

STRESS SIZE

lunch, I was glad I had invested my calories and money in a substantial meal. The day was only half over and I would need my strength to make it through the mountain of manuals that remained to be read.

Chapter 7

THE NEXT DAY I RECEIVED A PHONE CALL AT THE STORE FROM Alisha, the human resources director for the zone. I had never met her face to face, but she had facilitated my promotion as well as my transfer to Denver. I was indebted to her for all her help and hard work in getting me out there to the city with a stable job to sustain me.

She asked how I was doing with the training. It was only my second day, so I told her everything was going well. She made polite conversation, asking me how the move had gone and whether I was enjoying the weather. She then informed me there was a slight change in plans.

"Listen," she started. I could tell this was going to be something I didn't want to hear. "Jeff is being recruited to help out with some district manager duties in Houston."

"Oh," I replied, not quite sure how that arrangement would affect me and my training. "Do you know when he'll be leaving?"

"Soon," she replied. "Very soon—probably before the end of the week."

"Oh." That was very soon indeed. I started to panic. I had moved all the way out here on a whim. I couldn't bear to see my illustrious plans unravel. "Where does that leave me? Will I still be able to finish my training?"

"That's the thing. I hate to do this to you, especially with you having just moved out here and being so new to the training program, but we're going to have to move you to another store."

Oh, no, I thought. With all the tumult of the past few weeks, I wasn't sure I could handle any more changes. But I needed more details before I panicked completely. "Which store did you have in mind?"

"It'll most likely be the downtown store," she answered.

Those were the words I *really* didn't want to hear. Hadn't I made it clear during our initial phone interview that the downtown store was the one location I couldn't fathom working at? Out of the two dozen locations in the Denver metro, why did she have to send me to that one? Didn't she know it was unsafe for a young girl like me to be roaming around downtown Denver, entirely unaccompanied?

"Is that pretty much a for sure thing?" I asked nervously. Surely, there had to be another possibility.

"I still have a few things to work out with the manager over there, but it looks like that's where you'll finish off your training."

I didn't know the first thing about downtown, to which my haphazard adventure only a few days before could amply attest. I choked down my frustration and asked Alisha where the store was located and where I should park. Luckily, as she informed me, being a manager—even an assistant manager in training—at the downtown store meant I would get a free parking pass to the nearest parking garage for the duration of my training. The perk didn't exactly make me feel better about the unexpected and unwelcomed change to my training itinerary, but at least I could cross one concern off my long list of worries.

"Shawna is a great manager," Alisha assured me. "The store is pretty high volume, but it has a lot of energy. It'll be a better fit, too, than Jeff's store, because your home store is also high volume. You're going to love it downtown!" She probably wanted to get me motivated about the forced change, but her overly exaggerated enthusiasm betrayed her seemingly motivating words. I was going to hate it there.

With the first inklings of hunger pains creeping in, I knew I was going to need another cupcake to cope with the unfortunate news. This time, however, I at least resisted the urge to consume the cupcake in its entirety. I split the oversized baked good in half and saved the extra portion to take home for Raleigh.

The upcoming change was all I could think about as I attempted to focus on the day's required sets of modules. When I finally returned home later that evening, I couldn't hide the giant frown on my face.

"What's wrong?" Raleigh asked, his own face frowning out of concern. "Did you have a bad day at work?"

"They're sending Jeff away to Houston. I guess he's next in line for a promotion to district manager and he has to help out over there for a little bit."

"What does that mean? Are you still going to get to finish your training?"

"Yeah, but they're going to have to send me to the downtown store," I reported remorsefully, flinging my purse and container-laden plastic bag onto the dining table. Most of the containers were empty from having eaten lunch, and they rattled together as I threw them down. But I had forgotten that one of them stored the second half of my cupcake. The frosting smashed against the lid in all the commotion. I hurried to the kitchen to attempt to repair the damage.

Thankfully, Raleigh didn't notice I had massacred the surprise treat. He instead shared my disappointment at the unfortunate news. "Oh, no!" I heard him exclaim from the living room. "That was like, the one store you *didn't* want to go to!"

"I know!" I cried, cloistered in the kitchen as I attempted to reshape the frosting into a presentable mound on top of the cupcake. Some of my dismay subsided as I began to discuss the situation. After trying to keep my troubled feelings to myself while at work, it was refreshing to finally talk to someone about my concerns regarding the changes. I reveled in the sympathy.

"So, what are you going to do?" he asked. I had popped back into the dining room to retrieve the other containers, which required washing. Raleigh's eyes narrowed as he contemplated the situation, brainstorming any and all solutions to my unexpected predicament.

Unfortunately, there weren't any. "There's nothing I can do," I replied regretfully. "I'm going to have to train downtown." I had known I was taking a risk in putting my future in the hands of the company, but I had been so desperate to find a high-paying, stable job that I was willing to assume that risk. Now, I was going to have to accept whatever changes they made to the plans that I had formulated. The situation was beyond my control, whether I liked it or not.

Usually so carefree, Raleigh's voice now dripped with concern. "Are you going to be safe over there? What about the days when you have to get there really early or stay late? It'll be dark outside."

"Yeah, I know. That's exactly why I didn't want to be over there!" I yelled from the adjoining kitchen as I washed out the empty lunch containers. I couldn't sit as I carried out a conversation, even such a serious one as was taking place. I had to stay productive.

"Well, take my knife with you for protection!" he yelled. The suggestion seemed more like a demand as he strained to be heard.

Wiping my wet hands on my pants, I abandoned my dishwashing efforts and poked my head out of the doorway to peer at my husband sitting on the couch. He hadn't even bothered getting dressed. Nestled on the cushions in nothing but his underwear, he didn't strike me as the type of person that would condone the use of weapons. I didn't even condone the use of weapons. I didn't even know why he had a knife in the first place. "I'm not taking your knife," I scoffed.

"What are you going to do if some homeless man accosts you?" he speculated with raised eyebrows. He knew I possessed an irrational fear of being attacked. But in my mind, it was better to be safe than sorry. Letting down my guard was asking for trouble.

He had a point, but the thought of pulling out a knife, let alone having to use it, terrified me. With my luck, I'd end up haphazardly stabbing someone in self-defense and get arrested for attempted murder. Even more likely, however, was the possibility of hurting myself rather than my attacker. "I don't even know how to use your knife," I informed him.

"Here, let me show you." He leaped up from his comfortable corner of the couch and scurried to the bedroom. He rummaged through a pile of knickknacks thrown in the top drawer of his nightstand before pulling out his silver-colored knife with the white, pearly inlay. He flicked some switch on the side and the knife blade swung out to a sharp point. My eyes popped open wide with horror.

"I can't use that!" I insisted. I was weak and clumsy. I was going to hurt myself.

"Sure you can, it's easy." He folded the blade down and snapped the knife shut. He showed me the opening motion again, but it didn't look any simpler. It looked dangerous.

"I don't know about that," I said warily. "It's scary."

STRESS SIZE

"That's the point! It wouldn't be much of a weapon if it wasn't scary."

"Let me see it," I said, holding out my hand. Raleigh closed the knife and handed it to me. I fidgeted with it for a minute but I couldn't get it open. "I'm going to look like an idiot in front of my attacker trying to get it open!" I sighed heavily, handing it back to him for his assistance. He showed me the mechanism again, up close so I could really see how it worked. It almost made sense.

Raleigh gave me the knife again and waited patiently as I finally opened it. The blade swung out and nearly cut me open. With the way I handled that thing, I was going to do more damage to myself than my target! I tried opening and closing the knife a few times, but the action didn't get much easier.

"You just need some more practice," Raleigh assured me.

"I don't want any more practice," I responded. "I don't even want to use this thing!"

"Take it, honey. I want you to be safe."

"Fine..." I sighed. Another win for Raleigh.

I happened to have the next day off, so Raleigh and I took the opportunity to explore downtown. I at least wanted to familiarize myself with the area surrounding the store before having to report for work before dawn. I didn't want to get lost in the middle of some strange part of town, let alone in the dark!

We paid for parking at a nearby lot and walked into the store. With the entrance facing the pedestrian-infested promenade, the store was exceptionally crowded, especially for a weekday. Spread out among the wide, two-story sales floor, the store featured a remarkable selection of shoes, clothing, designer wares, and home goods—all at unbeatable prices. It was no wonder I had difficulty maneuvering down the aisles. The store was packed with shoppers looking to find a great deal.

In the midst of all the chaos, I identified one of the managers from her decorated name badge. "Celia," it said, printed in neat letters above various symbols highlighting her achievements and awards. She was busy trying to deal with a customer, who was flailing his hands and appeared to be unhappy for some reason or another. I waited for Celia to resolve the conflict before introducing myself.

"Hi, I'm Nicole," I said, extending my hand before she could call up the next customer. "I'm the new college recruit that will be working with you and Shawna for the next six weeks."

"Oh, yeah, they told me about you," she said in a nasally voice. She shook my hand hurriedly as she peered behind me at the mass of people congregated in front of the registers. "Nice to meet you," she added flatly.

I could tell she was stressed and probably wanted to help the next customer to get the line down, so I said, "Well, I wanted to stop by and check things out before starting tomorrow." I slapped a smile on my face even though Celia had been somewhat brusque with me.

"Well, thanks," she replied, already flagging the next customer over to the counter.

I stepped away from the counter and turned my attention toward Raleigh. He had been waiting for me a short distance away to allow me the opportunity to speak with Celia. "Well, now what?" Raleigh asked, walking alongside me as we exited the store. "What are we going to do now that we're here? It'd be a waste to drive home right away after coming all the way out here."

He had a point. Standing out on the street corner, we now faced the pedestrian-only avenue. I looked around and spotted a shoe store conveniently located across the walkway. Just the place I needed to visit. "Well, I do have those new shoes in the

STRESS SIZE

car," I said. I knew there was a reason I stored any and all of my lukewarm purchases in the trunk of the car. I never knew when I would run into the right store and be able to get my money back. "They're not comfortable, so I'm going to try and return them."

"Haven't you already been wearing them to work?" Raleigh asked. He wasn't one to cause a scene or try to stretch the rules to his advantage. He'd rather absorb the loss of wasted money on an unneeded purchase than create a conflict at the customer service counter. Whenever we had a return, I was the one who dealt with it. And, with my incessant indecision and nagging second-guessing, returns had become routine for me.

"Only two days," I replied. That was nothing in the grand scheme of things. One time, when I was still an associate, a guy had walked into the store with a pair of shoes he had worn for a year and insisted on getting his money back. In addition to being incredibly dirty, the shoes were encrusted with dried blood. But in a consumer-centric retail environment, he got what he wanted. Two days of gentle wear could be forgiven. "That doesn't matter," I insisted.

Raleigh scoffed with disbelief. "They're not going to take those back!" He was embarrassed that I was even considering the possibility.

"Sure they will! People do it all the time. The shoes aren't even dirty. Watch." I reveled in Raleigh's opposition, because the feat wouldn't be much of a challenge at all. I had worked in retail and customer service for most of my teenage and adult life. Customers can get away with almost anything.

"Okay," Raleigh replied, still not convinced. "But I'm going to pretend I don't know you." I rolled my eyes but remained silent. That was a typical remark for him whenever I attempted to stretch a store's return policy or milk an extra discount out of an already unbelievable deal. I knew my frugal ways embarrassed him, but my penny-saving behavior had gotten us this far, and I wasn't about to let up any time soon. Besides, what good were the shoes if I couldn't even wear them? I was much better off getting my money back and finding something that didn't sabotage my sensitive feet.

Raleigh reluctantly joined me as I retrieved the shoes from the car and walked back to the shoe store. "Do you even have the receipt?" he asked, still trying to talk me out of a potentially confrontational customer service situation.

I laughed at the ridiculous question. It was like he didn't know me at all. "I *always* have the receipt," I replied. Money was too precious not to save every proof of purchase. I needed some reassurance that I would be able to get my money back should something go awry or an item not work out.

Raleigh slowed down and entered the store a few seconds behind me, so it wouldn't look like we were actually together. He didn't even look in my direction as he headed to the opposite side of the store. He feigned interest in the end cap display as I handled the return.

The cashier pulled the shoes out of the box, checked the soles for any signs of wear, and asked me if there was anything wrong with the shoes. I smiled and said no, they just weren't what I needed. Sure enough, the unsuspecting cashier handed over my thirty dollars in cold, hard cash. Crisp bills in hand, I was satisfied as I exited the store. To make matters even better, I knew that with a little hunting, I could find a better deal elsewhere.

Unfortunately, returning the snazzy dress shoes meant I would have to report to the new store the next day in my dingy old sneakers. I'd been wearing those same black shoes for every shift since I started working for the company over two years before.

STRESS SIZE

The soles were worn out, and holes had begun forming in some of the creases. I was somewhat embarrassed about them, but at least they were comfortable. With my tight schedule and long shifts, comfort was of the utmost importance.

Besides, I seriously doubted that anyone was going to care about my raggedy old shoes. It was attitude, not necessarily appearance, that mattered. With my hardworking ways and desire to produce the best possible results in my new position, I was sure to make an impression. Something as frivolous as frayed shoes could be forgiven when I was about to make my mark in the management team.

Chapter 8

My alarm clock buzzed at the unseemly hour of 3:30 a.m. I groaned and stared at the neon green numbers glowing in the darkness. I reluctantly pulled my weary body out of bed. Waking up that early was essential if I was going to get ready in time to report for work by 5:30 a.m. The sun wouldn't have even had a chance to peek into the sky at that early hour. I'd be venturing into downtown before dawn.

I prepared for the day, attempting to make as little noise as possible to avoid waking Raleigh, who was entangled in a mess of bed sheets as he slept soundly. He was lucky that he didn't have to rise at such an obscene hour, but his slumber made my task of getting dressed all the more challenging. The flashlight became my best friend as I hunted through my top dresser drawer for a fresh pair of socks and underwear, and through the closet for a blue blouse and a black pair of slacks. The color organization of it all made the process of finding what I needed so much easier. I thanked myself for being compulsive about arranging my clothes according to the color spectrum. I had always known there was a reason for my madness.

Dressed in my uniform, lunch in one hand, purse in the other, I was ready to embark into what I still considered to be the night. Even though it was still summer, the air was crisp, and I could see my breath accumulate in small clouds as I exhaled. I was thankful for the large travel mug full of coffee that I had somehow managed to carry along with all my other belongings. The drive was quiet as I followed the directions listed on my printout. In the early morning hour, there were hardly any other cars on the road. The highway was wide open, just the way I liked it.

The morning was off to a good start, even if it was still dark out. Downtown looked different in the darkness, almost magical as the lights twinkled in the distance. As I approached the city center, I could see the fog rising from the small holes in the sewer covers, like small clouds in the otherwise sleeping and motionless section of town. The urban quality of dirt, construction, and cinderblock wasn't my preferred aesthetic, but it had its own appeal. I could learn to like it.

I felt so at peace at that moment that I almost didn't realize the danger of entering the parking garage. The entrance stood directly behind the light rail line, so when I saw the train approaching, I knew that I would either have to wait for it to pass or attempt to zip in front of it. I didn't want to be the cause of an accident, so I waited. What I didn't realize, however, is that the length of the stopped train would inevitably block the entrance of the garage. I waited several minutes before the train moved on, allowing me to finally enter the garage. I worried that I would be late, which would have been a tragedy on my first day at the new store.

The inside of the garage was surprisingly tiny. The width of the drivable portion between the rows of angled parking spaces was narrow, and I could tell from the thick black marks stretching across the walls that several vehicles had previously had trouble navigating the tight turns. Despite the early morning hour, there were few available spots. By the time I found one, I was almost on the top floor. I glanced around to observe my surroundings before exiting my vehicle, to be sure there weren't any strangers lurking about. I loaded my arms and shoulders with all the things I would need for the long day, and shuffled over to the elevator.

The overwhelming scent of urine wafted from the elevator as the metal doors slid open. I hadn't seen a stairway as I had navigated through the garage (not that I would have wanted to walk down five flights of stairs in the dark), so I had to endure the stench all the way down to the bottom floor. When the doors reopened at the ground level, I was shocked to see a homeless man sleeping right in front of the elevator. I dug out the knife that I had tucked away in my purse at Raleigh's bidding, worried that the man might wake up and attack me. He stirred slightly, most likely from the cold tiles lining the small lobby, but didn't awake. Even so, I had to step over him as I exited the elevator. I kept my knife in my hand as I crossed the street, just in case there were any other unexpected encounters.

Luckily, I didn't have to walk far. The store was across the street from the parking garage. Somehow, between having my purse slung over my shoulder, my lunch bag looped around my arm, my training binder pressed against my chest, and my coffee mug clutched by my free hand, I rang the buzzer along the side of the building. I waited. When, in a few minutes, nobody came up to let me in, I rang the buzzer again. It was cold outside, and I was still worried that someone might sneak up behind me. I didn't want to wait outside any longer than I absolutely had to.

Finally, a large woman with short, curly hair came up to the glass door. As she unlocked it and let me in, she apologized for the wait. She had been tied up with an unexpected phone call and couldn't come up. Still shivering, I smiled and introduced myself, perhaps unnecessarily since I was wearing my name badge. No sooner had I entered than she locked the door behind

STRESS SIZE

me and began walking through the store. She walked briskly, surprisingly so for her size, and didn't slow down as she talked. She introduced herself as Shawna, the store manager. She would be overseeing my training for the next four weeks.

"Only four?" I asked, confused and out of breath. My training was clearly scheduled to take place over the course of six weeks.

"I'll be gone for a week on a company business trip to open up some new stores in Chicago. Then I'm taking a vacation," she explained. She glanced at the concern spreading across my face. "But don't worry. You'll be in good hands. You'll be with one of the assistant store managers here. She's all prepped and ready to go to be a store manager. She's waiting on a position to open up at another store."

"Oh," I replied. That was a lot of information at once. I was still trying to adjust to the initial shock of yet another change in my training itinerary. The other extraneous details were overwhelming.

I had the opportunity to catch my breath as we waited for the elevator. She had ignored the stairs and headed straight for the less exhausting route. Had my arms not been full, I would have preferred the extra exercise. For now, I enjoyed the momentary break from the short sprint. The metal doors slid open with a faint chiming of a bell, and we stepped inside the oversized elevator meant to transport multiple shopping carts at a time. The old elevator squeaked and groaned as it crawled down into the basement. It paused at the bottom, doors still closed, and I wondered how many people had gotten stuck in that ancient piece of machinery. I shuddered and tried not to think about it.

We got down to the windowless basement of the store, half of which served as a sales floor, the other half of which was divided into an office, break room, and stockroom. Shawna led me to the office and invited me to set my purse down. She said that with the type of people employed at the store, that it would be safer locked up in the office than in the lockers in the break room. I thought this generalization was a little harsh and judgmental, but I took her suggestion nonetheless. She showed me to the break room, where I stowed my lunch in the communal refrigerator. She popped back into the office for a brief moment, then, wielding a portable scanning device, announced that it was time to accept the delivery.

Shawna was all business as she whisked me away to the loading dock. She barreled through the swinging double doors of the stockroom, nearly knocking me in the face on the rebound. She whizzed right past the young woman who was running frantically through the windowless, concrete room as she prepared for the morning delivery. "That's Becky, the stock lead," Shawna said in passing. I looked back at the girl struggling to pull out the portable extensions of the conveyor belt. Nobody was there to help her, and even Shawna had only barely glanced in her direction. Apparently, we didn't have time to stop.

We walked up a narrow set of stairs tucked away behind a locked door in the stockroom. The stairwell was cold, dark, creepy, and entirely unmonitored by any sort of video camera. I was thankful that only someone with a key, such as a manager, could access the area. It was the perfect place to commit a crime. But I felt much safer with this woman, no matter how little I knew her, than I had ever felt in the wide-open store with Jeff and the other male district managers. I was almost thankful to have been transferred to the downtown store.

When we arrived at the top of the stairs, Shawna grabbed the pair of scissors sitting on top of the small ledge protruding from the wall. She then pointed out the small monitor mounted in the corner next to the exit door. The screen displayed a couple of large dumpsters outside the door, but other than those trash receptacles, the alley was empty. "Always check the screen before you open the door," she warned.

"Why?" I asked, concerned.

"You want to make sure that the delivery truck is there before you go outside. It can be pretty dangerous. Sometimes there's a homeless guy sleeping in the alley," she explained.

My eyes widened. Homeless men sleeping in the alley behind the store didn't seem safe, especially not for me, who would have to venture out there in the dark to accept the morning delivery. "What am I supposed to do if there's a guy sleeping in the alley?" I asked nervously.

"You tell him to leave!" she exclaimed, as if that answer should have been obvious. Wielding the scissors, she was rather frightening. I imagined how an unsuspecting foe would be afraid of her. But even holding scissors, my thin frame wouldn't be a fair match against some homeless guy, let alone an angry one who was being forced to move from his makeshift lodgings. He probably didn't have anywhere else to go and would give me a hard time if I asked him to leave. I wouldn't know what to do in that situation.

Shawna spied me contemplating the hypothetical circumstance, and assured me that since I was only going to be a trainee at the store, there would always be another store manager there in the mornings. There might be days when I would have to accept the delivery by myself, but should a compromising situation arise, I could call for backup on a walkie-talkie. That was, of course, if I remembered to bring one with me. I felt somewhat relieved by this knowledge, but not much. The situation still didn't seem safe.

Based on the empty alley in view on the screen, the delivery truck hadn't arrived yet. Shawna looked at her watch and tapped her foot impatiently. "They're late," she complained. She was on a tight schedule and couldn't afford to waste even a moment. The tap, tap, tap echoed through the passageway. Finally, after several minutes standing awkwardly next to each other at the top of the stairs, we saw the truck arrive. She immediately pulled out the jumble of keys in her pocket to unlock the door.

Crisp air slipped through the crack of the door as Shawna peeked out to make sure the alley was free from any lurking strangers. With the coast clear, we squeezed out into the alley next to the truck. The morning sun, which crept up slowly into the sky, illuminated the smoke seeping through the truck's exhaust pipe. The city scene was rugged but almost pretty.

I had let my guard down too soon. Suddenly, a rancid stench hit me like a slap to the face. My nose stung with nearly singed nostrils as the smell wafted through the alley and permeated my senses. Whatever unpleasant odor I had withstood in the elevator in the parking garage, this repulsive funk was infinitely worse. The alley reeked of stale urine, old sweat, and rotten trash, only in a highly concentrated, incredibly lethal form. I doubled over and nearly gagged.

Shawna didn't even flinch at the stench. She commented that the smell was fairly mild that morning, since the weather was remarkably cooler than it had been a few weeks before. The summer and the accompanying heat had made it much worse, as it amplified the smell. I found it hard to believe that the odor could be any worse.

To compound my disgust, she pointed out the lock on the small door to the chute extending to the stockroom. "Be careful when you touch it. Sometimes the homeless guys pee on it," she warned. She gripped the lock with her bare hands as she unlocked the door and revealed the conveyor belt used to move the freight from the alley to the stockroom below.

My horror at my filthy surroundings intensified. I huddled deeper into my pristine pea coat, attempting to bury my nose in the collar to escape the putrid aroma still penetrating the air. The effort was of little use. Either the smell was clinging to the inside of my nostrils, or it had seeped into the wool of my coat. I couldn't escape it.

The truck driver and his delivery partner stepped out of the cabin. The driver was an older man, tall and lanky with dusty blond hair and a stern face. His partner, shorter and stockier in build, sported a small smile as he walked toward us. Unlike his much older counterpart, he seemed friendly. Both men were dressed in dingy jeans and worn-out T-shirts. Their outfits didn't suit the cold weather.

They teased me as I shivered in my thick, heavy pea coat.

"You must be new here," the driver said, laughing at the sight of me shivering in the alley. He seemed perfectly comfortable with his arms exposed to the elements.

"I'm from Arizona," I chattered.

His chuckle turned into an uproar, breaking the sour expression he'd had since exiting the truck. "Well, then, you're in for a heck of a surprise! Just wait until it gets below zero in the winter!" He nudged his partner, who instead of joining in on the laughter, provided a sympathetic smile in response to my dismay.

There was no way, absolutely no way that I could stand out there in the freezing cold, not to mention in the snow. I'd die of hypothermia before even getting the truck unloaded! I didn't have enough body fat to keep me sufficiently warm. I imagined that's the only reason why creatures like penguins survived the winter—they were encased in a thick layer of blubber that kept them warm and safe from the chill of the snow.

I was grateful that most other stores didn't take deliveries in a forsaken alley. With any luck, my home store would feature an enclosed loading dock to protect me from the cold.

Shawna didn't say a word, only frowned that we were making small talk when we should have been working. She pulled out the scissors she had tucked into the pocket of her windbreaker and cut the zip tie around the lock of the truck. She scanned the barcode with the scanner and checked the number printed on the label to ensure that it matched the number listed on the sheet clipped to the board that the driver had handed her. She pulled out her keys, and after much jiggling, jimmied it open. The shorter, more amicable man lifted the handle to roll up the door. A solid wall of cardboard boxes faced us.

I glanced at the clipboard Shawna had set down on the edge of the truck bed. According to the paperwork, there were well over a hundred boxes in the delivery. "That's a lot of boxes," I remarked, surprised at the extent of the freight.

"That's nothing," Shawna replied, unfazed. "Just wait until Christmas. The box count will be double that."

I gulped. Coming from a low-volume store in the middle of the desert, such box counts were unheard of. What Shawna's store would receive in one day during the holiday season would have been a whole week's worth of regularly scheduled freight at my old store. While still an associate at my old store, I had only ever worked in the stockroom briefly as a fill-in during the holiday season. That was a busy time for us, but even with the extra cartons, the freight only amounted to half the amount now stacked up in the truck. I knew I had all sorts of modules to prepare me for the transition to managing the increased workflow, but still.

The adjustment would be challenging.

Shawna pressed a couple more buttons on the scanner to prepare for the delivery. She explained that each carton would need to be scanned before being hoisted onto the conveyor belt. Every five cartons, the count on the scanner would need to be verified with the count the driver had tallied up in his head. It was a way of keeping track of the inventory and holding the appropriate party accountable for any errors.

The driver flipped the switch on the side of the conveyor belt to start the process. The other man, who had stepped into the truck, removed a carton from the seemingly impenetrable wall. He slid the box along the floor of the truck to the driver, who then lifted it, turned around, and shoved it down the chute. The box slid down the conveyor belt into the unseen stockroom below.

The two men worked quickly, and I understood why they opted for lighter, breathable clothing. They were on a time crunch and at their accelerated pace, coats would have weighed them down and overheated their bodies. Within minutes, the mountain of oversized cartons diminished. I was surprised by their speed and efficiency, especially since some of those boxes were as big as people. Filled with everything from shoes to apparel, home accessories to electronics, and designer handbags to gourmet foods, they were probably just as heavy, too.

The two-man crew worked so quickly that the conveyor belt clogged up. Becky's small, frail voice, which somehow carried up the chute to our ears in the alley, begged them to slow down. The driver, who had been ambitiously cramming the chute with the massive cartons, shouted that he couldn't. They were running late. They had to be at the next store and couldn't afford to slow down.

The four of us waited in the alley, now fully lit by the risen sun. I loosened my tight grip on the opening of my coat. I was relieved, but nonetheless disturbed, that I had acclimated to the horrendous stench. The driver folded his arms across his chest in impatience. The man in the truck wiped the sweat off his forehead with the back of his hand but said nothing. Shawna heaved with a deep sigh. She double and triple checked the box count on the scanner, as if the number on the illuminated screen might suddenly change. That would have been a cause for alarm and immediate action. But instead, we waited.

Finally, after several minutes of stewing in awkward silence, the conveyor belt suddenly revved back up. The two men hustled even faster to make up for the lost time. Shawna could barely keep up with their quickened pace as she attempted to scan the label on the side of each of the boxes before the driver heaved them onto the conveyor belt. There was a collective wave of relief when the last of the boxes were sent down the chute. We had made good time, all setbacks considered.

With all of the store's freight unloaded, Shawna showed me what papers I needed to sign on the clipboard, and where. She showed me how to secure the lock on the truck, using the new zip tie featuring the next number in the sequence. These protective measures would ensure the integrity of the remaining goods, which would be delivered to the next stores on the route. We thanked the two men, and the driver grumbled about the whole process taking too long. Shawna locked up the delivery chute and we squeezed through the gap between the wall and the truck to return to the building.

We walked back down the stairwell, and as we entered the stockroom, Becky emerged from behind a mound of plastic-wrapped apparel. "I can't keep up with all this!" she wailed in an Australian accent. With her face set in a frown, she looked like she was about to burst into tears. She was such a small,

STRESS SIZE

fragile-looking creature that I couldn't imagine how she could move all of that freight around the room, even with the assistance of the flexible conveyors snaking through the space. I saw that at least now, she was not alone. A couple of other associates had arrived to assist her with sending the boxes down the appropriate line to the relevant department, where they would later be sorted by other employees. I was glad for her, for that small blessing in the schedule. It seemed like too much work for one person to have to open up all those boxes and send them to the right area for optimum efficiency in sorting.

As the performance-driven manager, Shawna didn't seem to care. Offering little in the way of consolation, she urged Becky to hurry next time so the conveyor belt wouldn't get backed up. Time was of the essence, for the drivers who needed to complete their delivery route, and for us as a store that had certain goals to meet. Shawna reminded Becky that under *her* direction, the stock team had been performing poorly, and they couldn't afford any more setbacks. Every minute counted when the clock was ticking. They had to boost their scores if they wanted recognition from the district manager. Becky and her team needed to be quicker, more efficient, and less whiny.

Shawna turned briskly away and walked out of the room, leaving Becky to somehow manage the workload with a minuscule staff. I scurried behind, carefully dodging the swing of the double doors as Shawna burst through and headed for the office.

Becky and her frustration with the overwhelming workload remained in my mind. I reflected upon Shawna's callousness toward the stock lead's plight. The manager had made her particular style clear. She was very particular and demanded nothing but excellence from her staff. I feared for my own training, which, for the most part, she would be overseeing. I had always been a high performer, perhaps even overachiever, but Shawna's unbridled determination made me feel lazy.

Our differences became even more apparent as she showed me around so I could get a feel for her store's unique layout. I had a sense of how strict and regimented she was, but as she discussed the various organizational details of each department, I realized that she took company policy and recommendations to an unprecedented extreme. Her attention to detail was frightening.

The sales floor on the lower level was immaculate. All the men's shoes were spaced evenly apart on the shelves, their toes facing forward with the laces tucked in for a tidy display. The men's belts were sorted by brand, then by length—shortest to longest. The ties were arranged from lightest to darkest, according to the color spectrum. Not a single hanger was on the floor, out of place, or sticking out haphazardly from the apparel racks. And, of course, all the apparel was accurately sized, down to every last article of clothing, down to every last tag and sizing sticker. Very precise and very time-consuming.

The home department, which was situated on the other side of the expansive sales floor, was equally as meticulously organized. Everything that could be hung, such as gift bags, utensils, and pots and pans, was neatly pegged in the appropriate section. Categorized by type, larger items were carefully placed toward the front of the shelves for easy access. Oversized items, such as rugs and wall art, were arranged by size and neatly stacked behind secure metal braces. There was an organizational solution for every type of item. Not a single object was out of place.

Equally as impressive was the sales floor spread out upstairs, which was characterized by the extensive selection of women's apparel and accessories. Much like the men's shoes, the ladies' shoes were spaced evenly apart with the toes facing forward.

STRESS SIZE

Designer heels and tennis shoes were neatly organized on end caps for optimum marketability. The apparel was categorized and subcategorized into specific types of articles of clothing, then sorted by ascending size for the most efficient shopping experience. Designer handbags, which of course were organized from lightest to darkest, hung neatly on pegs. The luggage, which occupied most of the wall space behind the registers, was not only grouped by size, but replicated the color spectrum across the expanse of the wall. Everything was perfectly organized, and it would stay that way until the first of the customers arrived to disrupt the pristine order.

 I knew I was compulsive and organized with my own belongings, to which my closet and dresser could amply attest, but executing such precision on a grand scale seemed like an impossible feat. I quickly learned how Shawna could accomplish such undertakings—she was spoiled with an excessive amount of payroll and a number of full-time staff members who were each dedicated solely to a particular section of the store.

 There was no other way such fastidious work could be completed. The employees would spend each shift meticulously sizing, organizing, re-sorting, and re-stocking—all while avoiding being a hindrance to the shopping customers. When they had completed their section, they would start over from the beginning, because with the number of careless shoppers milling about, their work would inevitably be tampered with. Sometimes, if the store was particularly busy and they had to divide their time between recovering the sales floor and cashiering, they would have to stay an hour or two after the store closed to tidy the mess.

 Whatever frustrations I might have felt picking up after the shoppers at my low-volume, relatively slow store paled in comparison to what the associates toiling in this relentless, fast-paced setting must have felt. They worked hard, for minimum wage, for a corporate-controlled store that failed to recognize their painstaking efforts. They were nothing more than easily replaceable cogs in an unforgiving machine.

Chapter 9

THE TRAINING PERIOD WAS CHALLENGING FOR ME AS I attempted to find my voice as an assistant manager. The company's career ladder included several other smaller managerial steps with increasing levels of responsibility intended to make the slow and steady transition to such an important role more seamless and manageable. My adjustment to my new position might have been easier if I had taken the typical route. But, unfortunately taking that leap made the transition harder. I took a shortcut and jumped straight from being a lowly sales associate to being second in command of the entire store. I had six weeks to fill in all the gaps in my knowledge and limited experience. As I delved deeper into the training modules and corresponding activities, I realized that six weeks wasn't a lot of time. There was much I needed to learn, a sizable amount of which could only be accomplished through trial and error.

    A lot of the pressure to perform stemmed from wanting to make a good impression, especially on Shawna, who demanded such a high quality of work from her employees. I wanted her and the other managers to think I could succeed in my new role, so I pushed for the same level of performance from the staff once I had read most of the modules and was authorized to manage the workflow on the sales floor. With the omnipotent managerial clipboard in hand and a special moniker embellishing my name tag identifying me as the manager on duty, I was officially in charge of a staff of nearly fifty.

All that power and control was a big deal for me, having graduated from college a few months before. Not many people could say they had doubled their salary right out of school with such a prominent position. The promotion was a dream come true for someone like me, who valued stability and financial security above all else. What's more, I was finally getting to exercise my organizational skills in a position that granted me complete control over the store's operations. There was nothing quite as exhilarating as the prospect of being in charge.

I knew that I possessed the necessary organizational skills and perfectionist drive to succeed in my new role. All my compulsions and particularities had been preparing me for the position long before I had even received the promotion. But even possessing these characteristics, I wasn't prepared for the unfamiliar and daunting managerial responsibilities that lay ahead. The modules could only provide so much knowledge. What I really needed was some hands-on experience, and until I acquired that, I was destined to make mistakes.

Some of my errors were caused by my unfamiliarity with the particular forms and papers used to manage workflow. The clipboard itself, which featured three full pages of the daily schedule, was difficult to decipher. The lengthy schedule listed unfamiliar names and a complex matrix of breaks and lunches, timed down to the minute, with no room for error or overlap. It took me a couple of weeks to figure out who everyone was, and even then, with the confusing layout of the break schedule itself, I would sometimes forget to send an associate to their break on time. This meant I'd have to send the next person late too, since I could only have one person gone at a time. The delays certainly didn't

STRESS SIZE

go over well with the tired and overworked associates, who were anxious for their breaks.

In addition to my own inadvertent negligence, there was the issue of the lack of personal responsibility exhibited by the employees. Even if I did manage to send people to break or lunch on time, they inevitably wrecked my schedule. If an associate was even one minute late returning from a break or lunch, their tardiness would throw the whole break schedule out of whack. Sometimes associates would be as much as five or ten minutes late returning from a break, which unpardonably ruined the break schedule. I found myself hounding the associates when they left, to ensure that they would arrive back on time, and questioning them when they were late to see if they had a reasonable excuse for their blatant disregard for the company's time and attendance policy. They didn't see how important adhering to the schedule was for the store. They didn't see the big deal with being one or two minutes late, but one or two minutes quickly added up when there were twenty, or sometimes even thirty, associates on the clock on any given day. Meanwhile, the select few who were typically on time were forced to postpone their own break or lunch as the result of someone else's carelessness.

Managing the breaks and lunches wasn't my only concern as an assistant manager of a large retail store. The seemingly endless stack of papers attached to the clipboard outlined the sizing assignments and other projects that needed to be completed by the associates. After assigning each associate their respective tasks for the day, their work needed to be checked by me, and possibly redone if deemed unacceptable, before each of us could sign off on it. The actual signing off part was crucial, since that was the only way corporate could verify that the work had actually been done. If the little boxes next to the tasks weren't signed, it was as if the work was never completed. Between trying to match up the employees to the names listed on the sheet, to hunting them down to ensure they had completed their daily assignments, all while running up and down the stairs and back and forth across the sales floor, my head was spinning. I couldn't seem to keep up with every aspect of the store that required my constant attention.

In addition to struggling to grasp the store's particular methods for managing the staff and their assignments, interacting with the associates also proved to be challenging. The employees and I appeared to have different opinions regarding company procedures and quality standards. I only knew how I had worked as an associate, always going above and beyond my manager's expectation, and I foolishly anticipated that everyone else would exhibit the same steadfast dedication. Unfortunately, that wasn't the case. I was disappointed to discover that not everyone was as detailed-oriented and determined as me.

Even though that was the case, I still pushed the employees to be more like me, to work as hard as me, and to be as obsessive over details as I was. In all my fervor to excel, I was quick to make demands of my employees and slow to forgive when they made mistakes. I always pointed out what they did wrong, but rarely praised them for what they did right. And, as I had done on my first day of work at Jeff's store, I didn't hesitate to point out when an associate was breaking company policy or dress code. I had read all the rules several times, and I was under the impression that they needed to be strictly enforced. I wanted so desperately to make a good impression on Shawna and the district managers, that I took it upon myself to ensure all of the employees obeyed the rules.

My unyielding approach didn't earn me any friends, and my

desire to adhere to the same level of excellence demanded by Shawna was met with much resistance from the staff. Any time I said something, no matter how benign or mundane, the employees responded with scowls. If they didn't immediately frown in response to my requests, they blatantly ignored them. Sometimes I would have to remind associates of their assignments two or three times before they would finally get started, and even then they would do so with much reluctance. Slamming carts and flinging store merchandise became routine for the employees as they expressed their annoyance and frustration with me.

At first I couldn't understand why they were so hostile toward me. I had always been the type of person to do my absolute best with whatever job I had been assigned, and I couldn't comprehend why they wouldn't want to do the same. Their negative attitude toward work was so alarming that I became afraid to approach anyone about late breaks or dreary assignments, fearing how they might react if I had to give them some unfortunate news. I didn't want to be the victim of some angry outbursts.

My own ambitious attitude was undoubtedly responsible for much of the employees' negativity, but their undesirable behavior could have also been caused by a number of other issues. One of these was my age. Most of the employees were much older, perhaps even twice my age, and probably didn't appreciate taking orders from someone that they considered to be a baby. They might also have harbored some resentment toward my expedited promotion. Some of the associates had been working for the company for over ten years, and in some cases fifteen, and had long ago had their wages capped at a pittance without so much as an offer for advancement. And there I was, standing over their shoulders as an assistant store manager after only two years of service, telling them what to do and how to do it. Other employees might have been jealous that I was earning twice the amount of their minimum wage earnings without so much as lifting a finger to assist them with their seemingly endless list of assignments. My privileged position didn't seem fair.

For a while, I deluded myself into believing that after all my pain and struggling to make ends meet, I had earned the right to be handsomely paid to boss people around. After all, I had gone to college, and some of the associates had barely made it through high school. Surely my extensive education granted me some sort of advantage. But the more I thought about it, the more I realized that my authoritative position really wasn't fair. The company didn't care about their associates, or about me. They only offered the seemingly lucrative compensation package to managers to sucker them into squeezing every last ounce of utility out of the associates. The power structure was skewed and unjust, but that was the way corporate ran the system, and nobody dared to question it unless they wanted to lose their job.

The company pretended to care about their employees, to appease them and keep them quiet. There were some half-hearted attempts to reach out to the underpaid staff through the Employee of the Month and other recognition programs, sales contests with modest prizes, and a limited number of annually awarded scholarships to deserving associates. But the amount of money invested in these services was pitiful compared to the millions the company was raking in every day. Meanwhile, the associates squeaked by on minimum wage earnings and food stamps, sometimes holding down two or three different jobs to pay the bills. Their loyalty and service was being abused by the greedy corporation.

Ultimately, all the company cared about was making money. If that meant only paying minimum wage, or slashing hours on the employee schedule, or even laying off workers, then that was simply the price that needed to be paid in order to make a profit. They didn't care about health issues, childcare concerns, or scheduling conflicts. They only saw how much money these inconveniences cost the company. To corporate, the associates weren't people—they were cogs in the machine. They were easily replaceable, easily disposable parts.

I struggled with the inequality for weeks, especially when I realized the extent of the poverty many of the employees endured. Sometimes, a boy would sit in the break room for lunch with nothing in front of him because he didn't even have enough change to buy a snack out of the vending machine. Other times, a girl would call out of work right before the start of her shift because her baby was sick and the sitter had bailed out at the last minute. We even had a situation where a girl would go missing for days at a time because she was on the run, trying to protect herself and her kids from an abusive boyfriend or husband. Life was tough for the underpaid staff, much tougher than I had ever had it as a college student. They toiled at work, and they toiled at home, and they had nothing to show for their efforts.

Their struggles gave me a whole new perspective on how to approach them with compassion and understanding. As a self-proclaimed perfectionist, I often preferred to complete tasks myself to ensure that they were done according to my high standards. But there was simply too much work to be done, and I couldn't possibly do it all by myself. I needed help. I needed the assistance of the staff. In order to obtain their help with as little resistance as possible, I had to learn to let go of my own particularities and accept their sincere efforts as being sufficient.

It took some time, but slowly, I began to learn each of their strengths and weaknesses. Their skills I utilized to the store's advantage by scheduling assignments that they could complete quickly and efficiently. Their shortcomings I turned into training opportunities by providing specialized attention and additional resources where applicable. I praised each of the associates for what they did right, and when they were doing something wrong, I gently reviewed company policy and procedures with them and ensured that they clearly understood what was expected of them. I provided both verbal and written recognition for jobs well done, and also for effort, even if they didn't quite reach the goals that had initially been set out. I took a humane approach to training, tried not to judge, and treated each of the associates with the time and respect that, in all of the hustle and bustle of running an efficient store, they had never been shown before. After all, they were only human. They weren't pieces of machinery.

Most of the associates eventually warmed up to me, especially once I began to value them as people and openly recognize them for their efforts rather than calling them out on their mistakes. There were, of course, a few exceptions. There were still those whose resentment toward me remained resolute despite my remarkable shift in managerial style. I tried not to take their reactions too personally. Not everyone was going to like me, no matter how hard I tried to be an exceptional manager. I could only hold myself accountable for my own attitude and attempt to foster a sense of teamwork and achievement.

Chapter 10

ALTHOUGH MY CHANGE IN PERSPECTIVE TOWARD MY STAFF made many of my managerial responsibilities easier to fulfill, the physical demands of the job itself began to take their toll on my body. I often arrived early, stayed late, and went above and beyond the call of duty by working quickly while still ensuring optimal quality. My work ethic had the anticipated impact of improving the store metrics and performance scores all across the board, but the intense level of dedication was not without consequences. The stress of the position began to make me sick.

Having inexplicably lost fifteen pounds since the beginning of the year, I was already fairly thin for my height. However, with the long shifts, nonsensically rotating schedule, and the amount of exercise required by the sheer size of the store, another ten pounds melted away in just a couple of weeks. I thought maybe I was losing water weight, and didn't really think anything of it, until another ten pounds disappeared the following week. In less than a month, I went from being a passable, relatively healthy size to being nothing more than a walking bag of skin and bones.

Standing on the scale each day became routine as I tracked my rapid transformation into a skeleton. I preferred to check my weight first thing in the morning, after using the restroom but prior to eating, in nothing but my underwear for the most accurate read. Each day, the little red needle on the scale wheeled around to one mark lower than the previous day's reading. The steady loss seemed to be my only constant in my rapidly changing world.

I didn't even recognize myself as I examined my body in the mirror. At an unprecedented 115 pounds, I looked sickly and emaciated. I hadn't weighed that little since I was a child. Standing in front of the mirror, I could see each of my ribs protruding from the sides of my chest. My thighs didn't even touch when I stood up. My arms had lost their typical jiggle, and my wedding rings were so loose that I was worried that they were going to slip off and get lost. I was wasting away, and fast.

I knew I needed to regain some of the weight that had fallen off unexpectedly. But I couldn't eat. Nothing sounded good, nothing tasted right, and almost everything that I did eat made me feel sick. Sometimes, after forcing down a meager amount of soup or salad, I would walk up and down the pedestrian promenade to see if any of the fine foods being offered by the plethora of restaurants would strike my fancy. Nothing ever did. I would walk into a restaurant and stare at the menu, carefully reviewing each of the ingredients listed for each of the various options. I would always find some flaw or another regarding the food's preparation, and I would leave with empty hands and an empty stomach.

With my appetite virtually nonexistent, I resorted to eating handfuls of fruits and vegetables as a feeble attempt to consume an acceptable amount of nutrients. Carrots, cucumbers, and apples became my snacks of choice as I struggled with the nausea that usually followed whenever I could manage to eat something. But even then, that wasn't enough, because those foods cost more calories to consume than they actually contained. I continued to wither away.

STRESS SIZE

At first, Raleigh hardly noticed my extreme weight loss. He had always made it a point each day to say how beautiful I looked, but as I lost more and more weight, he never mentioned how my body was changing. It was only when I pulled his face in front of my protruding ribs that he became concerned about my weight. He began to monitor how much food I would take for lunch to ensure that I was taking an acceptable amount with me. But that was only if he was even up that early to see me pack my lunch. Most days I left the house before he was even awake, so he settled for my verbal reports as a way of tracking my caloric intake.

When I would call him during my lunch breaks to say hello, he would ask me what I had eaten that day. Sometimes, if I had been feeling well enough to choke something down, he'd congratulate my efforts. But other times, if he felt that I hadn't eaten enough, he'd encourage me to eat more. If the nausea passed, I would follow his advice. Most of the time, however, I resorted to leaving my leftover food in the refrigerator in the break room so Raleigh wouldn't see that I hadn't finished what small amount of food I had taken with me. I didn't want him to worry.

My loss of appetite compounded my sudden weight loss and transformed my body into something unrecognizable. The drastic change became even more apparent one day as I reviewed the footage on the security cameras at work for one of my training assignments. A toothpick came across the screen, and I asked myself, "Who's that?" Then I realized that the twig was *me*, and I became embarrassed by my own ghostly frame. Somehow I singlehandedly disproved the theory that the camera added ten pounds. It seemed to take it away.

The more weight I lost, the more my energy waned and my pace slowed from exhaustion. Waking up was a chore, getting ready for work was challenging, and actually making it through the day was painful. As my body entered starvation mode, my muscle mass began to deteriorate and I became incredibly weak and fragile. My bones ached, my muscles were sore, and even simple actions, such as walking or brushing my teeth, became exhausting. Working was impossible.

A particularly challenging circumstance arose during the stockroom portion of my training. To complete one of the modules, I was required to assist in the stockroom for at least three mornings. I was scared, because from what I had seen of the stockroom during my brief encounter with Becky during my first morning in the store, the stockroom was incredibly fast-paced and extremely stressful. I had only ever helped out in the stockroom once before, while still an associate at my old store, and that was with a different processing system in place. I was unfamiliar with the new setup, and as a result, my pace was remarkably slow.

My embarrassingly slow speed was additionally hampered by my lack of strength and energy. Even the most minuscule of tasks was difficult for me. With each of the joints in my fingers flaring with pain, I struggled to tear open the plastic bags that encased each article of clothing, secure matching pairs of shoes together with zip ties and other security devices, and stock the shelves with merchandise. I fumbled with the pushcart stacked with fragile goods as I feebly attempted to push it down the aisle. I nearly knocked several people over trying to roll the tall, heavy cart through the store. Everything I did, I did slowly—almost excruciatingly so. A turtle could have moved faster than me.

I barely managed to get through the first day of assisting in the stock room. By the second day, my body was so worn out from trying to process apparel from the mountain of boxes that had been delivered, that I could barely stand to finish the remaining merchandise, let alone get started with that day's freight. I had arrived early that day, much earlier than the start of the stock team's shift, and probably needed a break, but the stock team typically took their break together and I didn't want to disrupt the workflow by leaving the processing line. I kept working, much to my body's detriment. By the time Becky announced break time, I was seeing spots.

Hustling to process the piles and piles of merchandise in the stockroom was the least of my worries. At least in the stockroom, my focus could be narrowed to the task at hand. But working in the stockroom was only a training activity, a hands-on exercise to get a feel for the various types of work done in the store so that I could effectively oversee the efficiency of the processes. Managing store operations was an entirely different issue, one that required much greater skill and considerably more stamina.

With my strength utterly zapped, the multitasking required by my stressful position at work transformed into a herculean obstacle. As part of the activities for the training modules, I had to complete projects that would normally be done by associates, so that I could get the practice and understand the job. The assignments themselves, which often required bending, stooping, and heavy lifting, were physically demanding and therefore tiring. If those assignments had been my sole tasks for the day, they might have been manageable in my fatigued state. However, I never did only one thing at a time.

I was always doing at least two or three, and sometimes four or five, tasks at a time. I would be managing the break schedule, responding to phone calls and customer inquiries, monitoring store metrics and performance goals, and assisting on cash register whenever the line stretched out of control—all while trying to complete the side projects and other assignments outlined in my training binder. The workload never seemed to let up, and with my rapidly decreasing weight and failing health, it was even more taxing.

Part of the overwhelming workload was characteristic of the position itself, but some of it, and perhaps even most of it, was my own refusal to admit that there was anything wrong with me. I had always been so determined, so hardworking, so meticulous, that slowing down, even for a moment, seemed like failing. And I was still so new in my position that I didn't want the company to think they had made a mistake in promoting me. I wanted desperately to do well, to make a good impression, and eventually be granted my own store as a salaried manager. I saw only the prospect of the money that could be earned. I didn't value my health well enough to jeopardize that potential prosperity.

My perspective changed one day when the toll the position was taking on my body became brutally apparent. For nearly a week, the unpredictable Colorado weather had been alternating between mildly warm and piercingly cold. The first snow of the season had already fallen, and with the weather having trended on the cold side for several days in a row, Shawna went ahead and opted to have the heat turned on for the entire building. Unfortunately, the day after the technician showed up to turn on the heating system, the weather was warm outside, and the inside of the store became unbearably hot. The temperature made my strenuous tasks even more difficult to complete.

My body didn't tolerate the heat well. In the sweaty sauna of a store, I had a strict deadline to meet as I singlehandedly attempted to reorganize the entire young ladies' department, all while overseeing the break schedule and associate task list. I had only managed to eat an apple that morning for breakfast, so

STRESS SIZE

between not eating enough, pushing around heavy apparel racks, rushing to meet a deadline, and trying to manage an entire sales floor while being utterly too hot in the heated store, I started to feel faint. But I wanted to finish, and I ignored the blaring signals my body was sending. I pushed myself to get past the fatigue by moving faster, working harder, and testing my body's limits.

My refusal to listen to my body was a mistake. Dark spots clouded my vision as I started to pass out, and I clung to the unsecured clothing rack to keep from falling to the floor. Without the wheels locked, the rack rolled in the opposite direction, nearly careening into the woman pushing her cart down the next aisle. My own negligence had nearly injured someone. I clearly needed a break, so I told Celia, the other manager on duty, that I wasn't feeling well and asked her if I could go ahead and take my lunch. With me off the clock, Celia would be the only manager on duty, and I didn't want to abandon her without letting her know what was going on. She looked at the long line snaking around the registers and told me flatly that I would need to wait. The store was too busy for me to stop working, no matter how poorly I felt.

It was at that moment that I realized that even as an assistant store manager, a praised and supposedly highly valued employee, I didn't matter. My health wasn't important to the company. Corporate only cared about the contributions I could make to improve the company's bottom line. My health, well-being, and even my sanity would have to be sacrificed for the sake of the greater good—the greater good being increased profit. After all, that's what they were paying me for, to put the company first, even before myself.

I needed to change all that. I needed to put myself first, ahead of the company and all its rules and expectations, for the sake of my health and my sanity. No job was worth jeopardizing my well-being, no matter how much it paid. But making such good money, let alone being the only one in my household working, I couldn't bear to part with the compensation. I simply couldn't afford to.

As I struggled to make it through each day, I focused on what the company could offer me in terms of money and benefits. I couldn't quit, so I at least needed to focus on the positive aspects of my job. I didn't feel I had a choice other than trying to find the silver lining of the dark cloud looming over me. I continued to put my health at risk in order to pay the bills. After all, I had to be able to live, and I couldn't do that without money.

Chapter 11

THE AIR COOLED CONSIDERABLY AS THE SEASON TRANSITIONED from summer to fall. From what I could gather from the customers' comments, the remarkably cooler weather was a welcomed change from the record high temperatures of the summer. But for me, coming from the oven otherwise known as Arizona, the brisk temperature resembled a Tucson winter. I didn't have enough meat on my bones to properly acclimate to the rapidly dropping temperature. I found myself shivering nearly incessantly. The weather was another inconvenience to add to my long list of troubles as I attempted to adapt to my new, stressful life in a still-unfamiliar city.

In addition to bipolar weather, my waning weight, and my tumultuous adaptation to my responsibilities as an assistant manager, there were a couple of major disputes that arose in the workplace. First, there was the initial mix-up of my work schedule, which consisted of forty hours rather than the forty-five I had been promised in the job offer letter given to me by Alisha. Shawna, who had written the schedule and would be paying for my hours out of her store's payroll, disputed the clause, claiming that the additional overtime only referred to my permanent position at my home store, not to my initial training period. But there was no such distinction made in the letter, and I had moved nearly a thousand miles to a place I had never even seen before on the basis of that letter. I didn't particularly want to work the extra five hours, but I was counting on that money to help me get set up in my new home. I fully expected the company to honor their offer.

After much debating, Shawna reluctantly parted with the additional couple of hundred dollars a week to pay for the promised overtime. Unfortunately, she did so by cutting several hours out of the associate schedule each week. There was only so much money set aside for payroll, and with a potential legal dispute on her hands, she had to make a monetary cut somewhere. I regretted that the employment contract had to be honored at the expense of the employees, but I was already having a hard enough time settling into my surroundings. I didn't need financial complications to worsen matters. I hoped other opportunities would open up for them to make up for the lost time, and therefore lost wages.

In addition to the scheduling dispute, there was the issue of delayed health insurance enrollment. According to the job offer letter, and all the literature I had read regarding company policies and benefits compensation, the enrollment was to be immediate upon starting the position. But I never received my enrollment packet in the mail, and when I raised my concerns, all the managers at the store assured me it would arrive shortly. I allotted two or three weeks for the package to arrive, but when it still hadn't shown up, I asked again. They assured me that it would come soon, that I needed to be patient. Somehow I didn't feel so sure.

When by the end of my fifth week of training the package still hadn't shown up, I insisted that Shawna call Alisha to find out what was going on. The elusive human resources director didn't answer, so Shawna left a message. Alisha finally responded the next morning by emailing the contact information for the

STRESS SIZE

company that handled the benefits enrollment. Fortunately, I had the morning shift that day, which gave me plenty of time to pull up the information online when I arrived home later that evening.

I opened up half a dozen tabs on my browser detailing all the health insurance options, co-pays, and deductibles, but there was some sort of glitch in the system that prevented me from viewing my specific account information and the corresponding premiums. This information would have been outlined in the enrollment packet, but since I hadn't received it, I had to do all the necessary research myself. I wanted to know what I was paying for, and how much I was going to be paying for it, before I committed to a full year of coverage. That was my hard-earned money that was going to be deducted from my paycheck, and I wanted to be sure that the insurance coverage was worth the cost.

I needed answers, and since it was still fairly early in the evening, I went ahead and called the customer service number on the screen. It was lucky I did, too, because the woman on the phone informed me that it was the last day for me to enroll. I found this difficult to believe, since nobody had informed me there was a deadline, and it wasn't my fault I had never received the enrollment package. It hardly seemed fair that I should be rushed into making such an important decision at the last minute. She apologized for the inconvenience, but politely informed me that if I didn't want to wait until the next open enrollment period several months later, that I would need to make my decision by the end of the night.

I panicked. My window of opportunity was closing in a couple of hours. There were so many different types of plans, with different deductibles and drastically varying levels of coverage, that I didn't know what to pick. From what I could tell from what little information I had read prior to calling, the terms were confusing, and the amount of material that remained to be reviewed was overwhelming. There was no way that I was going to get through the hundred pages of enrollment information by the end of the night, and I couldn't make such an important decision without doing all of the necessary research. I was forced into an impossible situation of desperate decision-making.

The woman, who had been waiting patiently on the other line as I reflected upon the situation, asked if she could be of any assistance. I asked if it was at all possible for me to receive an extension. She said no, unfortunately not, since the deadline had been set by corporate and was therefore non-negotiable. I refrained from fully expressing my immense frustration as I calmly asked her for the premiums for each enrollment option. If I was going to be coerced into such a costly expenditure, I wanted to at least know the specifics. She provided the requested information and wished me luck as I continued my now frantic research.

I revisited each of the health insurance tabs I had opened, skimming through the pages and pages of material as I attempted to summarize the information to make the most educated decision given my limited amount of time. I honed in a couple of charts that appeared to provide the best possible synopsis of the complex health care plans. The charts made a stressful decision somewhat simpler.

Still, there was the issue of evaluating the relative value of the coverage versus the cost. Either I could pay more upfront in higher premiums in exchange for lower co-pays and a lower deductible, or I could pay less upfront in lower premiums but risk having to pay higher co-pays and a higher deductible should I need to visit a doctor. The exorbitant deductible was alarming and somewhat prohibitive, but it appeared to be better than the alternative. I could pay all of that extra money in higher premiums out of each and every paycheck and not even end up utilizing the lower co-pays or the lower deductible. After all, aside from my fatigue and unexplained weight loss, I didn't really get sick. I didn't feel the need to sacrifice a huge chunk out of each paycheck for services I might not even require.

After much deliberation, I settled for the plan with the lower premiums. I wasn't thrilled about the higher deductible, but at least with that option, less money would be taken out of each paycheck. Also, I could control how much money I spent on co-pays by limiting the number of times I visited the doctor's office. I figured I could wait until I was *really* sick, and possibly even experiencing an emergency, before seeking medical attention. Maybe that way, I could keep my medical expenses to a bare minimum.

Having finally made a decision, I redialed the number on the screen and received the same customer service representative who had assisted me during my initial round of inquiries. She asked me all sorts of information relevant to the enrollment process, and within minutes, I had successfully obtained medical coverage. After hanging up the phone, I exhaled with a huge sigh of relief. I felt as if I had accomplished a great feat, especially considering the amount of intensive research I had squeezed into an hour. I had always been independent and self-sufficient, but I felt a little more grown up knowing that I had my own well-paying job with health insurance benefits. All my carefully conceived plans for my life were finally coming together.

Unfortunately, the health insurance coverage wasn't effective immediately. It wouldn't kick in until the beginning of the following month. Until then, I was still completely without coverage. This concerned me, since I couldn't predict the future and any number of terrible things could happen to me that would require a visit to the doctor's office. However, I had been without insurance for months, and a few more weeks weren't going to kill me. Even though I was somewhat concerned about my sudden weight loss and my remarkable lack of appetite, I didn't feel that my condition required immediate medical attention. I crossed my fingers and hoped I wouldn't experience a life-threatening emergency for the next few weeks as I waited for my coverage to commence.

The temperature continued to drop, as did my weight, and it was the beginning of October before I realized that I hadn't had a period since the end of July. That was over two and a half months ago—before I had even moved out to Denver. I kept hoping my period would start so my mind would be at ease. Every time I felt a dull ache or a sharp stabbing pain in my abdomen, I thought for sure it was menstrual cramps. But my period didn't come, not even a drop.

Without a period to release the pressure building in my abdomen, the pains in my pelvis only worsened, becoming more frequent and increasingly excruciating. Sometimes, the poking in my pelvis was so severe that it affected my daily routine. I'd be crawling into bed after a hard day's work, only to be attacked by a barrage of stabs that rendered sleep impossible. Other times, the glands near my groin would swell up, putting pressure on the nerves and blood vessels traveling down to my legs, which made walking awkward and painful. I never knew that not having a period could cause so many other problems.

The severity of my typical menstrual cramps would have been a blessing compared to the sharp pain I was experiencing with the sporadic stabs. At least then, I could grimace through the pain knowing it would pass after the first day or so. But the pain that I was enduring was all the more excruciating because it was so unpredictable and disruptive. Every day I hoped and prayed for my period to come, to finally put an end to my misery and flush out my system, but my cycle never started.

After nearly three months without a period, I panicked, thinking for sure that I had cancer, or at the very least, that I was pregnant. Either possibility terrified me, but I immediately dismissed the more malignant of the conditions, thinking I was too young to have something as terrible as cancer. And besides, I had heard horror stories of particularly painful pregnancies, which would have explained the fullness and pressure in my abdomen, along with the incessant stabbing sensations. An unexpected pregnancy seemed to be the most likely cause of my curious condition.

Although that answer was simple, it was not necessarily welcomed. Getting pregnant would have brought my career to a screeching halt, and I couldn't afford that. I needed to keep working at my well-paying job so I could continue to live comfortably and save up money. I had big plans for my future, of saving up a hefty down payment for a beautiful house, starting a lucrative retirement fund, and eventually living off all the interest. Having a baby wasn't part of my life plan, at least not until I could afford to provide for it.

On the other hand, I almost wished the answer could be that simple. Being pregnant would have explained the recent waves of nausea and fatigue, and even the additional weight loss and lack of appetite I had been experiencing. Knowing the cause of my suffering would have been comforting in its own right. I wasn't ready to have a baby, but at least then I could rest assured that my anguish was only temporary. That was better than wondering when my health would improve, if ever. At any rate, I took an at-home pregnancy test to put my mind at ease. It was better for me to seek some answers than to continue to worry over hypothetical situations.

I actually found myself disappointed when the symbols on the small screen informed me that I wasn't pregnant after all. A negative test was reassuring for my new career and my financial future, but not so much for my multitude of troublesome symptoms. If I wasn't pregnant, that meant that there was something else going on inside my body that was causing so much pain and making my period late—possibly something serious or life-threatening. I wanted to know what.

Unfortunately, my health insurance was still weeks away from being effective, so I was forced to contemplate my concerns without the knowledge or expertise of a physician. Conducting internet-based research was of little consolation. All the forums and medical websites that I discovered outlined a number of horrifying causes—everything from infertility to hormonal imbalances to cancer. All my symptoms seemed to match perfectly with every one of those chronic conditions, which only deepened my concern. The worrying and the waiting, more than enduring the severity of the symptoms themselves, was what really bothered me. I sensed something was wrong with my body, and I wanted to know exactly what. Facing the unknown was detrimental to my health, let alone my sanity.

But even the unlikely possibility of finally getting to the bottom of my medical mystery left me feeling unsettled. From what I had learned about doctors from my previous encounters, they tended to treat the symptoms rather than investigate the reason behind them. Finding out the root cause of my ailments would be expensive and time consuming. I wasn't sure I was up to the task, especially given how busy I was at work. Plus I had other

STRESS SIZE

plans for my funds, like building up the nest egg I had always envisioned for myself. Shelling out hundreds of dollars in co-pays, lab tests, and prescriptions was not my idea of money well spent.

At any rate, I still had a couple of weeks to debate a visit to the doctor's office. Meanwhile, I continued to struggle to make it through each day. The ten-hour shifts at work were brutal, especially when I lacked energy and didn't have the stamina to withstand the long hours. I wasn't eating enough, and I wasn't sleeping well. My internal clock had a hard time adjusting to the wildly rotating work schedule. One day I would work the evening shift and get home late, but the next day I would be required to come in early in the morning to accept the delivery. The schedule didn't make sense, and it threw my system further and further out of whack.

Things at home were difficult too, especially with the quirks and peculiarities of adjusting to a different environment. As if working and dealing with my health wasn't challenging enough, everything in the apartment seemed to be breaking all at once. I had gotten an unbeatable deal on the rent, paying hundreds of dollars less for a much larger unit than what was being offered by other apartment communities, but the monetary savings was accompanied by a remarkable cost in convenience. I was starting to think that the cheap price wasn't worth all of the trouble.

First, there was the issue of laundry. There were only two of us living in the apartment, but somehow we seemed to accumulate a ridiculous amount of dirty clothing. Between the mountain of clothes and the pile of bed sheets that needed to be washed each week, doing laundry turned into an all-day chore. The laundry needed to be loaded into the hampers, carried down the stairs, and transported to the nearest laundry facility, all the way across the complex. The machines only took quarters, and with the number of loads we had to wash, it took a lot of them. The process got expensive quickly.

In addition to the exorbitant cost, the machines themselves caused problems. Sometimes, if too many people were running the washing machines at once, the entire laundry room would flood. Raleigh and I would return to switch our clothes over to the dryers, only to discover that we had to wade through two inches of cold water in order to do so. And half the time the dryers took our quarters yet failed to function properly. We'd come back when we expected the drying cycle to be completed, only to find the clothes still sopping wet. We'd spend even more money and even more time trying to complete what should have been a simple task.

The inconveniences posed by the laundry facility could have been bearable if that had been the only issue with the apartment. Unfortunately, it wasn't. The community itself wasn't as safe as I had hoped it would be. We hadn't even been living in the complex two days before a strange man approached me in the courtyard and started asking me personal questions. When I evaded his gaze and refused to answer, he began following me around the complex. It was only after I turned around and yelled at him to leave me alone that he finally walked away. I ran back to the apartment and cried for nearly an hour out of sheer terror.

In addition to this startling encounter, I had been leered at on more than one occasion while checking the mail or walking over to the laundry facility. I worried that one day, some creep was going kidnap me or follow me back to my apartment and attack me in my own home. Eventually, after being stared at for the fourth or fifth time, I refused to walk across the complex by myself anymore. I explained my concern to Raleigh and asked him if he would accompany me in the future. He didn't mind since he wanted me to feel safe. He didn't even bat an eye when I insisted that the apartment door remained locked at all times, even when we were both at home.

Fearing for my safety wasn't my only issue as I attempted to adjust to my new life at the apartment. As Raleigh and I quickly discovered, the inside of our particular unit turned out to be less than ideal. Problem after problem arose, which only heightened my stress level. I had enough trouble trying to pull myself together and do a decent job at work. I didn't need to tack on maintenance issues to my long list of worries. I was lucky we didn't actually own the unit—we would have gone broke trying to fix everything that went wrong with the place.

For starters, multiple light bulbs in the ceiling fixtures went out, including the bulb in the heat lamp in the bathroom. Trying to stay warm while sopping wet was challenging enough even with the lamp. Without it, drying off was a troublesome process comprised entirely of shivers. In addition, the front door was crooked, which not only made it difficult to open and close, but left an exposed, drafty crack at the bottom of the door frame. At least that crack stayed dry, but in the bedroom, the windows weren't properly sealed, which enabled moisture to accumulate on the sill whenever it rained or snowed. One time the gutter outside our window sprang a leak and all the nasty rainwater flooded right into our bedroom through the cracks in the seal. The room smelled musty for days as the water slowly dried out of the carpet.

To make the living situation even worse, the ceiling started dripping water whenever too much moisture accumulated on the roof. The drips wouldn't have been so bad if our bed hadn't been right under the leak. When I walked down to the office to bring the issue to the management's attention, Vince simply suggested moving the mattress. But moving the mattress wouldn't have solved the issue, and after weeks of my repeated maintenance requests falling on deaf ears, the drip turned into a steady stream. I came home one day after a heavy storm to discover that the leak had soaked the entire bed with dirty water. The water had seeped all the way down to the mattress. It took several hours to wash out of all of the water-stained sheets and dry out the mattress with a blow dryer.

Our troubles didn't end there. The pitiful excuse for a garbage disposal gurgled and moaned until it stopped working completely. At that point, it clogged up the entire sink with dirty, chunk-filled water and rendered the faucet useless for an entire weekend until the maintenance crew finally came out to fix it. Even worse was that the water for the entire complex would often be randomly shut off, with little or no advance notice. On more than one occasion, I was in the middle of cooking dinner, lathering my hands with soap to clean them in preparation for my next task, and nothing would come out of the faucet. And even when there was running water, the hot water was often freezing cold, which made showering before work impossible.

Nothing seemed to function properly in that dreadful place. It didn't seem fair. Of course, when I had conducted my preliminary research to investigate the complex, I had read all the tenant reviews. Some of the reviews seemed sincere, and others sounded grossly exaggerated and unfounded. There were several complaints about the management being ineffective and irresponsible, and even horror stories involving bed bugs. But the low rent was a seemingly good deal, and when I mentioned the bad reviews to Raleigh, he assured me that the tenants were probably overreacting and we weren't going to get bed bugs because we generally kept our dwelling neat and tidy. That was all the consolation I needed, and I pursued the rental application process despite the warnings listed in the reviews.

Valuing the low cost of the apartment rather than the amenities and overall maintenance was a mistake. Working was hard enough, especially in my fragile state, but living in that apartment made my life even more difficult. As the place fell apart left and right, I tried to focus on the positive by reminding myself of all of the things I liked about the apartment. This was challenging for me, since everything seemed to be going wrong all at once. But there was the high ceiling, the exposed beams, and of course, the fact that I even had a place to live. These were small blessings, but in the face of such troubles, they were all I had to be thankful for.

Chapter 12

My limited supply of optimism quickly diminished as attempting to balance my work and home life continued to take its toll. I was tired of being tired, sick of feeling sick, and fed up with everything that needed to be fixed in the apartment. The stresses of each day chipped away at my fragile sanity. I felt like I was on the verge of a complete breakdown. Hardly a day passed without my shedding at least a few tears.

Some days were harder than others. There was one instance that really set me off. I was getting ready for work and stepped into the shower, only to be immediately stabbed with ice-cold daggers of freezing water. I hopped out of the frigid stream and checked the lever. The gauge was firmly set on "hot," yet the water pouring out of the showerhead was unbelievably cold. The hot water wasn't working, yet again.

I snapped. After a late shift the night before, and another late shift awaiting me that evening, all I wanted to do was take a nice, warm shower. That didn't seem like too much to ask for, not when I had been feeling so sick and working so hard. But no, I was forced to suffer. Nothing could ever go smoothly or be simple. I shut the water off and stood in the shower, shivering, sobbing, and crying my eyes out.

Raleigh, who had been in the living room, heard my sobs and knocked on the bathroom door to check on me. After I didn't answer, I heard the door creak open. "Nicole?" he asked, concerned. "What's wrong?"

He couldn't see me cowering behind the colorfully striped fabric shower curtain. I liked it better that way. I wanted to wallow in my grief. After all, there wasn't anything else that I could do under the circumstances. Crying seemed like the only solution. He waited patiently me for me to answer as I continued to shudder from the cold and the sobs. I didn't want to answer—I wanted to put an end to all my misery. I wanted to die. But I couldn't afford to die. I had to go to work. I didn't have a choice. "There's no hot water," I finally wailed, my tears mixing with the water droplets on my face.

Raleigh gently peeled back the shower curtain to examine the severity of my emotional state. I avoided his eyes and hugged my arms to my chest, growing colder from the extensive collection of water droplets drizzled over my body. "Do you need to take a shower?" he asked.

"I haven't showered in days," I admitted, my lips set in a resolute pout. Between working and trying to catch up with the chores, I hadn't had the time. My hair was greasy and I probably stunk.

"So why don't you take a shower?" he asked gently, unaware of the extent of the situation.

"There isn't any hot water!" I cried with a fresh wave of tears. I couldn't possibly take a shower without any hot water. The water was too cold. I would turn into an icicle.

"Stay here," he said determinately. "I'll be right back."

I waited there in the shower for several minutes, cold and shivering. When he didn't return, I sat down in the bathtub and waited some more. Finally, Raleigh came in and engaged the stopper on the tub. I didn't understand his plan, so I asked him what he was doing.

"Don't worry about it," he said secretively. "It's a surprise." But I was worried, and I was cold, and I was completely pessimistic about my bleak life. I didn't think anything could possibly make me feel better. Clutching my cold bare legs to my chest, I simmered in my self-pity.

Raleigh returned again, bursting through the crack in the bathroom door with several pots of boiling hot water. "Stay back!" he warned. I nudged myself further into the corner of the tub. While running some of the cold water from the faucet, he poured the boiling liquid into the space. The resulting inch of water that filled the tub was a warm, toasty temperature. The heat was right, but the amount of water wasn't. I ran my fingers listlessly through the puddle surrounding me, wishing for more. A luxurious bath would have melted away my worries and thawed out my half-frozen body.

"Don't worry," Raleigh said, reading my mind. "There's more." He left the bathroom and immediately returned, carrying two more pots full of hot water. With the additional water, there was a small bath forming in the tub. That was better than nothing.

I settled for that fair amount, but much to my surprise, Raleigh wasn't finished yet. The supply seemed endless as Raleigh returned again and again with pot upon pot of hot water. He utilized the tea kettle and every pot and pan we had in the house. With the stove running at maximum capacity, he was able to boil enough water for a reasonably sized bath. Eventually, after the second round of boiling, I could lie comfortably in the tub with my body completely submerged. But even then, Raleigh didn't stop carting in water. Whenever the bathwater became even remotely cool, he had a fresh pot of hot water on hand to raise the temperature. My wish for a warm washing had been miraculously granted.

STRESS SIZE

Raleigh saved me that day from completely destroying myself with my own emotional turmoil. He saw me in one of my darkest moments and found something simple he could do to make me feel better. He even took his kindness to the next level by turning off the bathroom lights, lighting a few scented candles, and setting up the CD player on the counter with softly playing classical music. I sat in the tub and soaked, feeling relaxed for the first time in months. I didn't even care that I was spending an hour in the tub when I should have been getting ready for work. I needed that time to myself.

When I had shriveled up into a raisin, I drained the water from the tub and dried off. I felt peaceful and calm, so I took my time getting dressed. I didn't want to rush anymore, at least not then. I wanted to savor the sweet sensation of feeling completely relaxed.

After nearly an hour and a half of holing myself up in the bathroom, I emerged refreshed and renewed. Raleigh, who was sitting on the couch tinkering on his laptop, stopped what he was doing to look up at me. "How are you feeling?" he asked, trying to gauge my state of mind from the placid expression on my face.

"Better," I replied. I hadn't completely recovered from the cumulative trauma of all of life's stresses, but for now, regarding the most recent disaster, "better" was an apt description for how I was feeling. It would take months, and possibly even years, for me to fully adjust to all the recent changes in my life. I could only focus on the situation on hand.

"Do you want to talk about it?" he asked, inviting me to sit next to him on the couch by patting the seat cushion.

"No, not really," I replied. Too many unfortunate circumstances had accumulated in the past few weeks. As a result, too much negative energy had built up for me to talk about it all then. I didn't have time to sit down and discuss the full extent of my feelings and frame of mind. "Maybe some other time," I added, hoping that maybe someday, I would finally be able to talk about all my stress and frustrations. Maybe then I would finally start to feel well.

"Okay," Raleigh nodded slowly. He seemed to understand my sentiment without my having to fully express it, and didn't push for a further explanation. Sensing my stress level bubbling below the surface, he suggested I finally use the massage voucher I had purchased before we had moved.

With all the hustle and bustle of the move and starting my new job, I had actually forgotten about the voucher. The thought of getting a massage hadn't even crossed my mind as I had been struggling with the searing pain and debilitating weakness in my muscles. A massage would have been ideal to work out some of the soreness in my system. Of course, I would have to schedule an appointment. The sooner I could be seen, the better.

My eyes scanned the room for the nearest clock. The numbers on the microwave glowed with a surprisingly late time. I had spent too much time soaking in the bathtub. But I didn't want to risk missing out on the next available appointment, so I went ahead and looked up the phone number for the massage clinic anyway. As I dialed the number, I hoped the traffic wouldn't be bad on my way to work, so I wouldn't be late.

The phone rang twice and then a sweet voice answered, "Thank you for calling the wellness clinic. This is Stacy. How may I help you?"

She spoke so serenely that I was caught off guard. Nobody ever sounded that nice or that calm. "Hi … I have a voucher … for a massage," I stammered. The other end of the line remained quiet. "Do you have anything available tomorrow?" I asked.

"Let's see here," Stacy replied softly. She was so quiet that I heard the clicking of the keyboard as she looked up the appointment schedule on the computer. The clicking ceased and she said, "We have some availability in the evening. What time would work best for you?"

I paused. Morning would have been ideal. The evening was questionable. A fuzzy recollection of an important event taking place in the evening floated into mind. I had the whole day off, but I had a nagging feeling it wasn't a good day to be traveling on the freeway. I couldn't quite remember what was going on. Meanwhile, Stacy waited patiently on the other end of the line.

Then I recalled the flashing sign on the freeway. Bright orange letters had declared that there was a presidential debate tomorrow evening. The entire freeway would be shut down for security purposes. The closure would make traveling across town inconvenient. I would have to take the streets if I wanted to go anywhere. Still being so new to the city and having never been to that part of town before, I couldn't fathom taking the streets. Printed directions were helpful, but only if I didn't make a wrong turn. And with the freeway being closed, I imagined the streets would be backed up with the additional traffic. The last thing I wanted was to get lost or get stuck in traffic and be late to an appointment I was paying for.

"What other slots do you have?" I finally asked. "Do you have any morning appointments?" I wanted to see what all my options were before I booked a risky appointment time.

"We have morning appointments next Monday through Thursday," she answered. "What day would work best for you?"

I wasn't sure. I was hoping to be seen the next day—I hadn't considered booking an appointment that far out. With the hectic, rotating work schedule, I wasn't even sure what days I was working that week. I pulled out my schedule from a stack of papers on the desk and aligned my finger with the second week on the calendar. My nose scrunched up with frustration as I realized that none of those days would work for me. "I'm working next Monday through Thursday," I informed her. "What about next Friday?"

"I'm sorry, dear. We're only open Monday through Thursday, nine to one and three to six. We're closed for lunch from one to three, and we're closed on Fridays, Saturdays, and Sundays."

"Oh," I sighed. With tomorrow not being a good fit, and the following Friday being impossible, it didn't seem like I would ever get in for a massage. I was beginning to get discouraged.

Stacy wouldn't allow me to wallow in disappointment. "Well, what other days do you have off that you would be able to come in?" she asked.

I scanned the spreadsheet, eying the days marked with a little "x" to denote my time off. Unfortunately, my only days off were the very days the clinic was closed. The next available coinciding day was at the very end of the month. That was nearly four weeks away. My muscles pulsed with pain to remind me of how badly I needed to book an appointment. I grimaced and wondered how I could possibly wait that long. "It looks like the only day I can come in is the last day of the month," I finally answered. "Do you have anything available that day?"

"We're pretty much wide open that far out," she replied softly. "Is there a particular time of day that would work best for you?"

"Morning," I replied. The mornings were good. I could get the massage done and out of the way and have the rest of the day at my disposal. No time wasted.

Stacy asked me for my name, address, and telephone number, along with the number printed on the voucher. I answered all her questions, relieved to have finally found an available slot.

With my appointment set, I hung up the phone and let out a long sigh.

Bittersweet relief. I wished my work schedule wasn't so crazy so I could have been seen much sooner. The pain made patience impossible.

Chapter 13

MY SIX WEEKS OF TRAINING AT THE DOWNTOWN LOCATION finally came to a close. Although I had grown accustomed to the urban setting, and actually looked forward to getting fresh air each day during my lunchtime ventures along the promenade, I was glad to finally escape the long drive and the rush-hour traffic. It was time for me to settle into my home store, which was much closer to my apartment. The closer location would save me some much-valued time by cutting my drive in half. The permanence would provide some much-needed stability in my tumultuous life.

As much as I was looking forward to starting at the new store, I was nervous about meeting the staff and having to adjust to the store's particular setup. Getting used to the downtown store had been challenging enough, and by the sixth week of training, I had grown accustomed to it. Even some of the surliest of the employees were regarding me with flat faces rather than full-on frowns. I was finally making headway with the staff on my arduous journey as an assistant manager.

Now I was being uprooted all over again and plopped into yet another unfamiliar territory that would require additional adaptation. I didn't want to make all of the same mistakes all over again. At least this time around, I wasn't entirely lost and alone. I had the distinct advantage of having made connections with the

STRESS SIZE

managers in my training store, who were knowledgeable about my home store and familiar with the staff there. Before Shawna left for vacation, I took the opportunity to pick her brain about the store's setup and performance so I could gauge the amount of stress and work I could anticipate.

"It's a big store," she told me as we paused to tidy up a section of apparel as we surveyed the destroyed state of the sales floor. It was unusually cold outside, and the increased shopping traffic from the pedestrians seeking refuge from the weather resulted in a particularly picked-over selection. "It's also a two-story store, but it's even bigger than this one. It does more in sales, too," she said, spouting off some rather obscene sales figures.

Before my managerial training, those numbers would have scared me. After all, I was coming from a comparatively tiny store from deep in the desert of Arizona. But now that I had endured the ruthless retail environment of the centrally located downtown store, I felt prepared for the absolute worst. Alisha had been right after all that the downtown store would be a good fit in preparation for my more permanent position at my home store. Had I stayed at the sleepy little store far out north of the metro, those figures would have had me shaking in my worn-out shoes.

Celia heard that I was poking around for additional information about my home store, and despite our previous differences, was kind enough to offer her own inside knowledge. She informed me that when she had moved out to the city to work for the company, Donna, the manager of my anticipated home store, had overseen her meager three weeks of training. She said that Donna was "surprisingly cool." Determined and demanding, but as one of the youngest store managers in the entire company, she had an edge about her. Celia also said that since she had been so new to the city, Donna even offered to let her stay at her home until she was able to get settled. Letting a complete stranger stay in her home seemed like an excessively generous gesture, so I hoped for the best and that Donna would be as nice as she sounded.

Unfortunately, Celia had painted a bit too rosy of a picture of the store manager. When I reported for work early in the morning on the first day at my home store, Donna barely said hello. I already knew who she was, but she didn't even take the time to introduce herself. At the time, I was fighting a cold and could barely talk, but a simple exchange of formalities would have been appreciated. She was all business as she walked briskly to the back of the store, fully expecting me to follow. "We've got to take in the morning delivery," she shouted back to me, not even breaking her pace. She led me to the stockroom.

I hardly had a moment to catch my breath, let alone take off my coat or set down my purse, before the tall blonde woman handed me a portable scanner and said, "I assume you know how to use one of these." I did, since I had regularly assisted with the deliveries at the downtown store, but my login and password hadn't been set up in her store's system. Donna rolled her blue eyes, entered in her own information into the scanner, and got me started scanning the boxes as the truck driver hoisted them onto the flexible conveyor belt.

Fortunately, my wish for an interior loading dock had been granted. I didn't have to stand out in the cold to accept the delivery. But even with the back of the delivery truck pulled up to the dock, the crisp morning air crept in through the cracks along the edge of the expansive opening. The concrete walls of the stockroom intensified the chill. The cold air pierced my lungs as I struggled with the congestion in my chest. The skin of my frozen hands began to crack and bleed. My body convulsed with shivers. I bit my lip to fight the pain and continued scanning to keep up with the fast pace that had been established by Donna and the driver. I didn't want to slow down and make my new manager think I was weak and useless. I needed to make a good first impression.

There didn't seem to be any end to the stream of boxes. From the amount of freight being delivered, I could tell that the store was as high volume, if not more so, than the downtown store. I couldn't imagine how the driver mustered up the strength to hoist all of those boxes by himself. At least at the other store, the two men worked as a team to get the job done. I was exhausted just scanning the boxes. I wasn't even doing any of the heavy lifting.

Finally, the mountain of boxes diminished. We had finished the delivery. All the corresponding paperwork looked the same as it had at the other store, which was one less thing that I had to get used to. I was grateful for even that small blessing. I signed the papers, and since I didn't have keys yet, Donna locked up the truck and secured the new zip tie. With our managerial tasks in the stockroom completed, Donna left the stock team to process the products. She led me to the elevator and showed me to the office.

It was still early in the day, and the store hadn't even opened yet. Donna plopped down into an oversized rolling office chair and let out a long sigh. With the way she barreled into the morning tasks, I didn't think she was the type of person to take a break. My instinct was right—she wasn't. That sigh was the extent of her rest as she immediately dove into the day's agenda.

"Okay," she declared loudly, barely allowing me enough time to set down my belongings on the empty desk on the other side of the room. "We're going to get started with the morning paperwork. But first, grab a seat." Her tone was so insistent that I rolled one of the other oversized chairs next to hers and sat down without saying a word. Not that I could have emitted more than a whisper or two anyway, at least not with my voice stolen.

"Before we get started, I need to tell you a few things. I'm Donna and I'm the store manager here. I've been working for the company for seven years and I've worked my way up all the way from the bottom. I was a temporary, seasonal employee when I started, and now I'm one of the youngest store managers in the entire company. I only got to where I am by working hard and expecting others to do the same. I don't tolerate slacking, and I don't deal with drama. I'm here to work, and I'm here to make money. I'm not the type of person that's going to sit here and talk about how you're feeling, because frankly, I don't care. If you have any personal issues, keep them to yourself. We're running a business here, not a therapy session. Okay?"

She was so brutally honest that I didn't know how to respond. I tried to speak, which resulted in a loud rasp. I shut my contagious mouth and nodded to acknowledge that I had heard her. That ended the one-sided conversation. She logged into the computer on the desk in front of her and started the morning paperwork, complete with full commentary.

As I silently listed to Donna describe her preferences and particularities regarding company policies and procedures, I wondered how she would feel if she knew how poorly I felt. She seemed so strong, both physically and emotionally, that I didn't think she'd appreciate having such a sensitive and sickly assistant manager. I also wondered how she interacted with her staff, since she seemed so demanding and I had adopted such a human approach to managing store operations. But since it was only

STRESS SIZE

my first day in her store, and she had made it very clear that she didn't care to discuss our feelings, I kept the fragility of my condition to myself. Donna was my boss. She was not my friend. If I had any questions or concerns, I'd have to find somebody else to talk to.

Chapter 14

Shawna had been a tough and demanding manager, but Donna harbored even less tolerance for mediocrity. She had no qualms about expressing her disappointment with unsatisfactory performance, sometimes brutally so. On more than one occasion, she stormed into the stock room and launched into a tirade about how to properly process the merchandise for maximum efficiency. She also refused to hear excuses as the cashiers tried to explain why a certain customer had complained, or why their bagging and scanning scores were far below company goal. All she cared about was results. She wasn't interested in the reasons why she wasn't getting them.

Donna also made it very clear that she was unhappy with the training I had received at the downtown store. She often threw me into unfamiliar situations, such as checking off the work of the janitorial staff or executing the modified layout for the following month's marketing promotions, expecting me to fully understand what I was doing. But I didn't, and when I asked for clarification regarding the processes, she'd roll her eyes and mutter something about incompetency or incomplete training. I tried not to take her criticisms personally, since there was only so much that I could learn in six weeks. If there were gaps in my knowledge, it was likely the fault of the curriculum or the manager overseeing my training. I had done my best with the

STRESS SIZE

materials I had been given. Ultimately, it was the company's responsibility to ensure that I was amply prepared for my new position. As a salaried representative of the company, Donna took it upon herself to virtually retrain me.

My new manager was not only particular about certain processes, but she was also a diehard perfectionist. She'd give me an assignment, sometimes a physically intensive one, and upon witnessing my painfully slow pace or lack of strength, she'd hop in and take over the entire task. She preferred to do everything herself rather than to have someone else do it differently, or worse, incorrectly. She never seemed to run out of energy as she hurried tirelessly across the sales floor and up and down the stairs, switching from one task to another seamlessly and without error. She was the epitome of speed and efficiency, and despite all of her callousness, I admired her for those productive characteristics.

Eventually, I became accustomed to Donna's abrasive personality, and as far as the staff was concerned, I had a much easier time interacting with them than I had with the associates at my training store. I had already learned my lesson the hard way when I had quickly and naïvely assumed control without gaining the trust or respect of the people over whom I had authority. I needed to take the time to evaluate the various strengths and weaknesses of each of the employees before exercising my managerial skills. That was especially important at my home store, since I would be working here for the foreseeable future. I couldn't afford to butcher my relationship with my staff before it even started—not if I had any hope of being successful at this location.

My quiet observation served me well, especially since I continued to battle a cold and the accompanying loss of my voice for the first three weeks at my new store. Donna thought I was too shy and timid, and told me so when I didn't immediately take charge of the break schedule or the steadfast enforcement of the rules, but I stood my ground. Apart from using my illness as an excuse not to talk, we possessed completely different managerial styles. I wasn't going to pretend to be somebody I wasn't, even to impress her. Fortunately, when she saw how quickly her staff warmed up to me and my tender approach, she recognized the validity of my sentiment.

I slowly assumed more responsibility as the associates came to know and respect me. They realized that I recognized their unique talents and abilities, and that I valued and respected their contributions to the store. But more importantly, I *listened* to them. While Donna was coldheartedly professional, never talked about anything that didn't directly pertain to the store's operation, and expected her staff to work relentlessly and tirelessly as if they were parts of a machine, I saw the associates for what they really were—humans. I took the time to see how they were doing, and to lend a sympathetic ear when things weren't going well. I felt that connecting with the associates on a personal level was the most effective way to foster productivity.

At first, they'd gab for five or ten minutes at a time as they unleashed a flurry of pent up emotions. They hadn't really been encouraged, or even allowed, to talk at work before. If Donna was around to witness the encounter, she'd tap her foot in impatience or look around at the clock to see how much company time we were wasting. She didn't see the investment in time and personal interest as productive or beneficial. But it was. Once the associates understood that I cared about them as people, not just as employees, they didn't feel the need to talk so much and their performance significantly improved. They *wanted* to work for me, because I cared about them and their individual success. Donna saw her already impressive scores and store metrics rise even higher, and she stopped giving me a hard time about my approach.

The other assistant manager, Ted, commended me on my unprecedented personal approach, and for adhering to my managerial style despite Donna's initial opposition. His reassurance was comforting in the midst of the performance-driven manager's high standards and strict demands. While Donna was typically a closed door when it came to discussing issues and ideas, Ted was wide open. I found that I could talk to him about any of the dilemmas that arose as I adjusted to the store's particular setup and clientele. That support was comforting, especially as I continued to strive for excellence while still nursing my fragile health.

Ted was almost like a protective big brother as I settled into my new role at the store. He watched me as I worked while sick with a cold. He was impressed that I hopped right onto the cash register and helped out with the long lines despite being unable to communicate with the customers in anything other than soft whispers. But he also saw how weak I was, how tired I would get, and how despite being a skeleton at a mere 115 pounds, I wasn't eating enough and continued to shrivel up. He told me I worked too hard, and that I needed to take care of myself. I simply shrugged and kept pushing myself. The work wasn't going to let up simply because I wasn't feeling well.

There was one day, as I was nearing the end of the second week of my cold, that I felt particularly unwell. My throat glowed red and burned like a raging fire, and my voice, which had been slowly recovering, nearly completely disappeared. I was so tired that each of the joints in my body ached, down to every last finger and toe. Muscles I didn't even know I had were swollen with pain. I needed to rest, but I insisted on working. I had the evening shift, and everyone was counting on me to fulfill my responsibilities as the closing store manager.

The fever that consumed me had rendered me so delirious that I stumbled and nearly toppled over as I attempted to organize some of the hangers that had accumulated under the registers. Ted took one look at me, and at the two dozen hangers I had dropped all over the floor, and insisted I take a break.

"But I already had my last break," I croaked, slowly stooping to pick up the mess that I had made.

"I don't care," he said with deep frown. "Take another one." He signaled for me to stand aside as he picked up the rest of the hangers.

I crawled at a snail's pace across the sales floor and up the stairs to the office. Nestled in one of the cushioned rolling chairs, I rested. A slight sense of guilt lingered as I drifted out of consciousness. Even though it was for the sake of my health, I was clearly abandoning my duties, and that left me feeling uneasy. The guilt didn't last long, and I nearly fell asleep as I sat in the quiet office for the next ten or fifteen minutes. I had temporarily escaped all of the stresses of the store and was alone in my own little world of sickness. That was something to be savored while I had the patience and understanding of Ted to support me. Donna would have never allowed that.

The sound of the office door opening forced me to open my eyes. Ted had arrived to retrieve his coat. It was the end of his shift and he was leaving for the day. I would be the only manager on duty, left to oversee the operations of the entire store as I battled the fever waging war inside my system.

"Are you going to be okay, kid?" he asked with his leather jacket in hand. He was at least ten years older than me, so I didn't mind him calling me "kid." It was nice to have somebody watching over me in the workplace, not judging me in my moments of weakness and questionable health.

"I'll be fine," I whispered. It was a lie, and he knew it too by the way he arched his eyebrows questioningly. I felt like I was dying, but I didn't want him to worry about me as he left the store to go home to his life outside of work. It wasn't his fault I was sick. There was no reason for him to bother himself about it.

"You've really got to take better care of yourself," he warned as I stayed glued to the chair. "I know you want to make a good impression, especially on the boss, but you're going to make yourself really sick if you're not honest with yourself. You've got to speak up when you're not feeling well. There's nothing wrong with being sick, or taking an extra break if you need it. Trust me, I know."

"You do?" I asked, dubious. From what I had seen of his unwavering stamina and ability to tackle any situation in the store, he was as driven as Donna, but he was more approachable.

"I do," he replied, still standing over me as I stayed huddled in the chair. "Do you know what lupus is?" he asked.

"It's an autoimmune disease, or something," I murmured.

"Yeah, well, I have it. I was diagnosed with it when I was about your age. At first, I didn't want to admit that I was sick. I kept doing what I was doing and I didn't take care of myself. Then I got *really* sick. I lost so much weight they had to put me in the hospital. Once I faced my illness and started taking medication, I started to feel better. Now I go months without getting sick, and that's because I listen to my body. I can sense when I'm pushing myself too far, and then I know that I have to take a step back. If I don't, I'll end up in the hospital again."

"So, you're saying that I have lupus?" I asked, still trying to adjust to the fact that he had shared something incredibly personal about himself. I didn't see why he was telling me about his battle with a chronic condition. I understood why Donna had made such a big deal about keeping personal issues tucked away—they could get awkward.

"Right now, you probably just have a fever. But you never know, and you don't want to wait until you're stuck in the hospital before you find out. Don't let this job destroy you," he warned. "It's only a job."

"Okay." I managed to nod. It wasn't "only a job"—it was *the* job, the job that I was counting on to help me earn loads of money so I could finally achieve all my goals. Whatever it was that was making me sick would pass. I'd get over it and be back to my usual self, and then I could really shine. But I didn't want to bog Ted down with all of those details, so I said goodbye and wished him well as he headed home for the night.

He probably meant for his story to serve as a warning of what might happen to me if I didn't slow down and take better care of myself, but it inspired me to keep working. I lifted my body out of the chair and forced myself to walk back through the store. If someone with such a debilitating autoimmune disease could be an assistant manager, then so could I. Being sick would have to be put on the back burner. I had a job to do.

Chapter 15

EVENTUALLY, MY FEVER BROKE AND MY VOICE RETURNED. I regained some of my strength, but not much. My muscles were still incredibly weak. I had a hard time performing routine tasks in such a bustling retail environment. Exhaustion became the norm, but there wasn't anything I could do about it. I kept working through the pain and fatigue. I was thrilled when my long-awaited massage appointment finally arrived. I had certainly earned that hour of pampering.

By that time, Raleigh had begun private tutoring. I was glad that after being unemployed for nearly two months, he was finally getting out of the house and earning some money. Unfortunately, his new part-time position posed a challenge when it came to carpooling. The two of us shared the car, and with me working such a hectic schedule, it was difficult to coordinate transportation. When the day of my appointment arrived, I found out that he had inadvertently booked a tutoring session during the time that I would need the car to return home. He couldn't cancel his appointment, so he offered to take me to my massage and pick me up after he was done with his student. That meant I would have to remain at the clinic for an hour after my massage while I waited for him to pick me up.

Despite this inconvenience, my body quivered with excitement. I couldn't even remember the last time I'd been that enthused about something. My muscles were tied up in such tight knots that I couldn't even stand up straight. The session would give a whole new meaning to "massage therapy." My muscles needed some serious attention.

It was the end of October, and a light dusting of snow had collected on the ground. The cold only compounded my shivers of excitement. Raleigh pulled the car into the parking lot and dropped me off near the office. I braved the snow through the courtyard and burst into the lobby, all smiles. "Hi, I'm Nicole," I said loudly, hardly able to contain my excitement. "I have a massage appointment."

"Welcome," the woman behind the counter replied softly. "I'm Stacy. Please have a seat, dear. We have a few forms for you to fill out before we get started," she said as she handed me a clipboard with a couple of sheets of paper. She was so quiet, the ambience changed when she spoke. The air in the room felt softer, warmer. I felt calmer, yet nonetheless guilty for having announced myself so enthusiastically. The knob that controlled the volume of my voice clicked down several notches.

"Thanks," I almost whispered, overcompensating for my faux pas. I took a seat in one of the upholstered chairs in the waiting room as I filled out the form.

The clinic was so small that I could see it in its entirety from my seat. There was a room with an examination table and an x-ray machine, two smaller rooms with much lower examination tables, and another room with a closed door. Situated next to the chairs in the waiting area were three wobbly-looking leather seats with armrests. There were also three ropes set up along the wall that looked like nooses.

A lady and her daughter walked into the office, smiled and said hello to Stacy, then sat in the wobbly chairs. They looked strange as they repeatedly swiveled their hips in the chairs. The seats followed the motions of their bodies. It was awkward to watch, but I assumed that they knew what they were doing. I looked away when they got up and stuck their necks through the loops of the ropes on the wall. That was too painful to observe.

Apart from the strange equipment, the clinic was cozy and intimate. The office was quiet, even with the other ladies in the room and the gentle alternative music drifting from the speakers in the ceiling. The receptionist hardly made a sound as she shuffled some papers and clicked around on the computer. I felt like my pen scratching on the form was making too much noise. The peaceful environment was soothing. The massage hadn't even started yet, and I already felt more relaxed.

The form asked a lot of personal medical questions regarding my pain, muscles, and other symptoms. I filled out the questionnaire with everything that was wrong with me, since I didn't know which symptoms were related or could possibly be alleviated by massage therapy. I felt like I was writing a whole novel about my ailments as I filled out the form. Once I finished, I checked the form for completeness and handed it back to Stacy. She smiled and thanked me.

My wait was over as the massage therapist emerged from the adjoining room. "Hi, I'm Elena," she said, shaking my hand enthusiastically. The space around her appeared to glow as she smiled sincerely and energetically. I could tell by looking at her that she possessed an inner peace and happiness that radiated from her body. It was contagious.

"Hi, I'm Nicole," I responded with a huge smile.

"Are you ready for your massage?" she asked excitedly.

"I am *so* ready," I replied. I followed her into the room from which she had emerged. The small space was dimly lit, with a string of lights suspended from along edges of the ceiling providing a hint of luminescence. Flutes played softly in the background from hidden speakers. The air in the room smelled sweet, like succulent flowers. The whole ambience was very soothing. A wave of serenity washed over me.

"Have you ever had a massage before?" she asked, closing the door for our initial consultation.

"Once, about a year ago," I admitted. I was way overdue.

She nodded and smiled with a sense of understanding. "So it's been a while then. Do you know what you'd like to work on?" she asked. "Would you like a full body massage, or is there a particular area that's bothering you?"

"Oh, gosh," I blurted. Everything hurt. I didn't even know where to start. My neck and shoulders pulsed with pain. Those two areas were probably the worst. "There's definitely some tension in my neck," I said. I rubbed the area with my hand for emphasis. I could feel the inflammation burning underneath my fingertips.

"We can start there," she suggested, "and if we have time, we can move on to the rest of the body. Sound good?"

"Sounds great!" My face broke out into a giant smile. This was going to be money well spent.

"Okay, so take your time, we'll start face down. I'll be back in a few minutes."

"Thanks!" I replied. Elena left the room to allow me privacy to undress. I tucked my belongings in the cubby out of the way, and slipped under the crisp white sheets on the massage table. With my face pressed into the donut-shaped headrest, I closed my eyes and deeply inhaled the sweet scent of the room. Even the headrest was beautifully scented. The whole room reeked of relaxation. Between that and the gently playing instrumental

STRESS SIZE

music, I nearly fell asleep as I waited for Elena to return.

Within a few minutes, there was a soft tapping on the door. "Are you ready?" Elena asked.

"Yes," I replied, nearly in a trance.

She stepped into the room and closed the door behind her.

She folded the sheet down to reveal my back. Her hands were warm as pressed on my shoulders. "You poor thing," she said as she attempted to straighten my body. "Your back is so messed up!"

"What?" I asked, appalled that she would say such a thing to a stranger, let alone a client. I knew I had issues, but her remark offended me.

"Your back is so crooked!" she explained. "Your spine is like an 'S.' It's crazy!" She traced the zigzag of my spine with her fingers.

"I have scoliosis," I told her. "I inherited it from my mother."

"You should really see Dr. Johnson," she suggested as she started to gently rub the muscles of my back.

"Who's Dr. Johnson?" I asked.

"He's the chiropractor who works right here out of this clinic. He could really help you out."

"Oh, I don't know about that. It seems like an awful lot of money for someone to pop my back." I could think of a million other things that I would rather spend my money on than seeing some quack.

"Well, the first visit is free. He does free consults and x-rays."

"Huh," I grunted. That seemed too good to be true.

"Seriously," she said. "They're really good here. They'll totally work with you and your insurance. They're not in it for the money. They really care about helping people out."

"I don't know," I said, still skeptical. "Chiropractors aren't even real doctors. What if he messes me up?"

"Your back is only going to get worse if you don't get it checked out," she replied. "And besides, chiropractors have as much training as medical doctors, and at least here we're not trying to drug you up to get rid of the pain. We eliminate the cause."

"I see," I replied flatly, wanting to focus on the massage, which was actually starting to hurt as Elena started to dig deeper into the muscles. "I'll think about it."

I had been anticipating a relaxing massage, but the more Elena worked out the tension knots in my neck and shoulders, the more it hurt. But it was the good kind of hurt, the kind that meant that I was on the path to healing. Elena also talked during the entire process, asking about my education and interests, where I worked and why I moved to the city. At first I found the talking to be distracting, but I hadn't talked that much to anyone other than Raleigh since before we graduated from college. The outlet was refreshing and much needed. Between the massage and the pleasant conversation, I could feel my body releasing all of the toxins it had been bottling up.

The hour seemed short. My upper body was in such bad shape that Elena didn't even have time to work on any other sections. When the session was over, she left me alone to get dressed. She handed me a cup of water when I walked out of the room. "Make sure you drink plenty of water today," she warned. "You'll feel sick to your stomach from all of the nastiness being released from your muscles if you don't."

I thanked her and handed her a generous tip. I felt a little sick from the release of all of the lactic acid, but already I could tell that much of the swelling in my muscles had gone down. I felt lighter, more relaxed. She had worked a miracle on my muscles in less than an hour.

I sat in the waiting area and sipped on the water as I read a book and waited for Raleigh. Stacy kept looking at me with a sweet little smile, asking me if I was okay, or if I needed anything. Each time I said no, I was fine. Finally, after the third inquiry, she suggested taking advantage of the free consultation and x-ray as I waited for my ride. After all, it was free, walk-ins were welcome, and there was no commitment to pursue treatment. At that point, I was so tired of waiting around that I went ahead and said yes. My back was already so messed up that it couldn't possibly have been made any worse. I figured I had nothing to lose.

Chapter 16

THE INITIAL CHIROPRACTIC CONSULTATION CONSISTED OF A series of x-rays and tests. First, I had to pee on a strip, the changing color of which would determine the toxicity of my system. Then, I had my heart rate measured while resting, then immediately after standing up, which would identify any adrenal fatigue. Finally, I stood still for a set of two or three x-rays, which would be analyzed to determine the curvature and alignment of my spine. Dr. Johnson, a short and pleasantly energetic man, informed me that he would review the results that evening and I could come in the following day to discuss them with him.

When I returned to the office the next day before work, Dr. Johnson revealed the x-rays and the test results. He explained to me that according to the colored test strip, my system wasn't toxic. However, my stress level, as measured by my body's response to standing up after resting, was less than ideal. According to his findings, I was eating right and drinking enough water, but I was so stressed out that my body wasn't even sending the proper signals anymore. That statement seemed to summarize my life pretty accurately.

He then showed me an image of a ridiculously crooked spine, which snaked down the screen in an exaggerated "S." The twisting shape looked painful. There was no way that was an image of my spine.

"Is that me?" I asked, skeptical.

"That's your spine," he replied.

"No way," I responded, mouth agape. I knew that I was in a lot of pain, but I didn't think my spine was *that* bad. "How did that even happen?" I asked. I knew that my scoliosis probably had something to do with it, but as an adolescent I had been told that the curvature wasn't severe enough to require surgery. I thought I could go my whole life without having it looked at again.

Dr. Johnson pulled out a model skeleton and explained how the spine acts as a spring to keep the body balanced. When a patient doesn't maintain proper posture, or in my case, has a condition like scoliosis, the vertebrae become unevenly spaced or misaligned. That means that the "spring" doesn't function properly, which puts an unnecessary amount of stress on the spine, and even other parts of the body. Chiropractic adjustments ensure that the spine maintains its correct position, which fosters overall health.

That made sense, but I was still unsure about how seeing a chiropractor could help me. I had always been under the impression that chiropractors weren't real doctors, and that it was dangerous to be treated by one. Plus, it seemed like an awful lot of money to shell out to have my back popped. "What happens if I don't get treated?" I asked. I needed to know exactly what I was dealing with and whether or not it would be worth my time and money to seek treatment.

Dr. Johnson clicked around a couple of times and pulled up another image on the screen. The other patient's spine was so bent out of shape that the form was barely recognizable. That type of curve had probably crushed all of the internal organs. "This is a much older woman, who also had scoliosis," he said. "She had a perfectly straight spine after seeking treatment, but then she didn't see a chiropractor for ten years. She was in so much pain that when she finally went back, this is what her spine looked like. She needed surgery to get it fixed."

My jaw dropped even lower. The prospect of spinal surgery was terrifying. I didn't want for surgery to become a requirement, not when reaching that point of severity appeared to be preventable. But still, I didn't want to commit. "How many visits would it take for you to fix my spine?" I asked.

He clicked around again and pulled up my own x-rays for reference. "For someone in your condition," he said, "I'd want to see you twice a week to start."

"Twice a week?" I exclaimed. "I was thinking one a month!"

"It takes a lot of work to get those bones properly realigned," he informed me. "I'd want to see you twice a week for three months, then take another x-ray to see where we're at. Then we might go down to once a week for another three months."

"I don't understand why I would need so my visits," I contested. My mind was already calculating how much money all of those visits would cost, and how much time I would have to spend commuting and actually getting the adjustments. Hundreds of dollars, and hours and hours of my time were going to have to be poured into saving my spine.

"The muscles have a tendency to pull the vertebrae back to their incorrect position, because that's where they're used to being," he explained. "If you don't come in often to get your spine used to the correct position, you'll never really make any progress. Your body will keep reverting back to its misaligned state."

I still wasn't convinced. "What is all that going to cost me?" I asked. I wanted more details before I committed to such extensive treatment.

Dr. Johnson flipped through a folder and pulled out a sheet.

STRESS SIZE

The form had been filled out with my personalized treatment plan. My insurance, which happened to be effective as of that date, only covered the first twenty visits. After that, the co-pay would increase to the out-of-pocket cash price. It was well over $1,000 for the full course of treatment. Even with my well-paying job, I couldn't afford that. I had other plans for my money, like saving up to buy a house.

But I couldn't afford surgery either, which would have been the alternative if I refused treatment and allowed my scoliosis to take its toll on my spine. I was forced into the difficult position of choosing my health over my money. Feeling the pangs of panic seize control of my senses, I excused myself from the room. I called Raleigh on my cell phone to seek his opinion.

"Do what you need to do to be healthy," he said. "Even if it costs a lot of money, you wouldn't have to pay it all at once, and surgery would cost a lot more. You don't want to let it get that bad," he warned.

He had a point, but I still wasn't sure. I returned to the examination room, still undecided. Dr. Johnson sensed my reluctance and offered to honor the insurance price for the extent of my treatment. That knocked a couple of hundred dollars off the total price tag. He also offered to do the first adjustment for free, just so that I could see how it felt. That was better than committing to treatment that I hadn't ever experienced before, so I agreed to at least try it before making up my mind.

Dr. Johnson instructed me to lie face down on the examination table. The cushioned table had two lowered armrests and two bars in which to situate my face. With my arms resting and my face pressed into the headrest, I straightened myself up as best as I could. As far as I could tell from all the tugging Dr. Johnson did to my leg, I was much more crooked than I had envisioned.

He told me one of my legs was actually half an inch shorter than the other! No wonder my hip always felt like it was out of whack.

He felt along my spine, paying particular attention to the lower vertebrae, which, after years of leaving the scoliosis untreated, had become unevenly spaced to accommodate the irregular curvature. He pressed a lever along the side of the table and the lower portion of the table popped up unexpectedly. He pressed it again, only this time, while rolling his palm over my lower spine. The intense amount of pressure was somewhat painful, even more so when he started pressing on my back to stretch out the rest of the spine. I could barely breathe.

I was relieved when he asked me to turn around and lie face up, because I could finally breathe. But I had let my guard down too soon. He rolled his stool behind me so I couldn't see him as I lay staring up at the ceiling. He felt the bones in my neck, and apparently discovering one that was misaligned, held his finger in that spot as he shifted my head in the opposite direction. I heard a loud cracking noise as the gases released from the spaces between my vertebrae. I thought for sure he was going to break my neck, but I tried not to panic as he repeated the procedure on the other side.

After all that trauma, the frightening process wasn't even over yet. My neck was properly adjusted, but there was still more work to be done along my spine. Dr. Johnson asked me to turn onto my side. He bent my top leg and tucked my foot behind my bottom leg. He pressed down on my bent knee. Several pops resonated as my spine realigned, more pops than I had ever heard all at once. My eyes were wide with shock.

When he was finally finished, he asked me how I felt. I stood up, feeling lighter and taller, but nonetheless disturbed by the whole procedure. "I feel weird," I admitted.

STRESS SIZE

He warned me that since my body wasn't used to being properly aligned, that I might feel sick the first day or so. Unfortunately, I had to go to work later that evening. I felt weak and sick to my stomach during my entire shift as my body attempted to adjust to the new alignment. As if that illness didn't fuel my skepticism of chiropractic, the muscles along my shoulder blades hurt worse than they ever had before. Trigger points the size of olives formed, tucked under the bone, as the muscles in my back pulled on my properly aligned spine to return to it to its incorrect position. I could hardly stand up without experiencing some sort of pain.

When I went in for my next visit, I made a point of expressing my concern regarding the effectiveness of the treatment. Healing shouldn't have hurt that much. He assured me that everything I was experiencing was completely normal, and that the symptoms would subside after a few more adjustments. I could only arch my eyebrows in response.

Dr. Johnson didn't let my doubts dampen his enthusiasm regarding the effectiveness of chiropractic. He took the time to show me how to use the strange equipment set up in the lobby, which I learned strengthened the muscles along the spine to allow them to hold the spine in place. At first, I struggled to get the hang of the figure-eight motion of the swiveling chair, but I could feel the action exercising the muscles in my lower back. Stooping along the wall with my head stuck in a rope also made me uneasy, but the awkward-looking position maintained the proper curve of the neck to optimize the "spring" function of the spine. Combining exercises with the adjustments made a lot more medical sense than simply popping my back, so I stuck with the program despite my doubts.

And Dr. Johnson was right—after a few more adjustments, I stopped feeling so sick after the visits. Occasionally, if I had a particularly rough week at work, my muscles would flare up with pain, but I had earned some free massage time by referring Raleigh for a free consultation, so I was able to get some of the additional tension worked out. When I expressed my concerns about the excessive cost of combining massage therapy with the chiropractic adjustments, Elena confided in me that she only worked there at the wellness clinic part-time. She had her own massage facility on the other side of town. She encouraged me to seek treatment regardless of cost, and that if money was an issue, we could work out a special rate. She cared more about my health and well-being than she did about making money, so I took her up on her generous offer.

Squeezing in visits to Dr. Johnson's chiropractic clinic twice a week and to Elena's massage therapy sessions at least once or twice a month was unbelievably stressful in the midst of my already hectic schedule, but the effort was well worth it. I couldn't put a price or a time stamp on my health. After several months of suffering, I felt like I was finally on the track to true healing. Not only did my posture improve, but some of the other terrible symptoms that I had been enduring improved as well. I almost felt guilty for having doubted the integrity of alternative medicine when I had originally purchased the massage voucher that brought me to the facility in the first place. The wellness clinic was helping me in more ways than I could have ever possibly imagined.

For one, some of the numbness and tingling that I had been experiencing in my arms and legs subsided. Elena, who was sincerely passionate about her line of work, took massage therapy to a whole new level by showing me a few simple exercises to loosen my muscles and release the trapped nerves. I didn't have the time or the patience to commit to doing the exercises regularly, but they helped whenever I got too tense and the strange sensations returned. After a few minutes of following her instructions, the numbness and tingling would fade away. It was a do-it-yourself type of miracle. I needed that, especially when I was beginning to lose hope that I would ever feel completely recovered.

Elena, with her steadfast optimism and unwavering belief in my ability to heal myself, also turned into more than just my massage therapist. With how regularly I received massages, she became my friend and confidante. Sometimes, my muscles were so relaxed from my previous visit that I didn't actually need to be seen, but I kept my appointment anyway to fill her in on the recent events of my life and see how she was doing. I found that we had a lot in common, including an obsession with health, nutrition, and spirituality. After spending several months in solitude, I had found a kindred spirit. That discovery worked its own magic as I continued to strive for a complete recovery from my nagging weakness and fatigue.

Apart from the much-needed conversation provided by Elena, one of the most beneficial results of my treatment was that my missing period miraculously re-appeared. This was especially surprising, since utilizing my new insurance coverage to seek the attention of a gynecologist hadn't been effective. Like the other doctor I had seen at the beginning of the year regarding the same issue, she had merely shrugged it off as a "normal" side effect of stress. Since I was still working as an assistant manager and my stress level hadn't diminished, the chiropractic adjustments must have been the cause. After all, the only change to my routine was visiting Dr. Johnson. That being the case, I knew that there had to be a connection between my recent adjustments and the long-awaited arrival of my menstrual cycle.

Fighting my embarrassment regarding the sensitivity of the

matter, I asked Dr. Johnson about the correlation during one of my visits. He explained to me that all the nerves of the body stem out from the spine, and if the spine's not properly aligned, the nerves get pinched or the signals get crossed. Other organs in the body, including the uterus, won't function correctly if they're not receiving the proper signals. With the spine properly aligned, the nerves send the necessary signals, and the organs function appropriately. He didn't seem at all embarrassed to be discussing my menstrual cycle with me, and actually thanked me for being so candid with him. Remarkable cases like mine were the reason why he was invested in that type of business to begin with.

Between the chiropractic visits, the massage therapy, and my steadily improving condition, it was all starting to make sense. I didn't need doctors, medication, or surgery to make me feel better. I needed to pay more attention to my body and what it was trying to tell me. I needed to surround myself with people who genuinely cared about me and my well-being, experts like Dr. Johnson and Elena, who could guide me with love and care as I continued to pursue optimal health. A full recovery wasn't impossible as long as I continued to protect the health and integrity of my body.

Chapter 17

As the holiday season approached, the store's operating hours extended late into the night to accommodate the additional shoppers. The added stress of the increased workload and the even crazier schedule caused my symptoms to worsen. The relapse disappointed me. I had made so much progress on my path to healing, and it was being destroyed in a matter of days. But I couldn't very well quit the job that had brought me out to the city, even to protect my health.

With the hectic holiday hours, I squeezed in my appointments with Dr. Johnson and Elena. However, since I was destroying my body faster than I could repair it, trying to fix my back and massage my muscles weren't enough. I couldn't maintain my health and sanity when I wasn't listening to my heart. I wasn't being true to myself. I was forcing myself to continue working in a position that yes, I was good at, but wasn't right for me. There was only so much of that tension that my body could handle before it quit on me completely.

Despite all my best efforts and good intentions, I continued to waste away. All my strength was zapped. I was awake and painstakingly walking, but my mind and my body felt like they were asleep. Days floated by, and entire weeks passed before I realized that I hadn't really been living my life. I had been working, working, working—not even taking the time to sit down and talk to Raleigh, to enjoy a nice meal, or even take a much-needed shower. The store had consumed me. It had chewed me up and was getting ready to swallow me down.

I didn't even know who I was anymore. As an art student in college, I had once been so fun-loving, creative, and imaginative. But now, as I continued to deny my own physical limitations and push my body's increasing fragility, I had lost sight of my personality. I had abandoned all my wild dreams and haphazard endeavors in favor of practicality and frugality. In effect, I had lost my humanity.

In seeking out such a prominent and lucrative position, my quest for control had actually controlled me. I had been so desperate for achievement, for excellence and unbeatable performance, that I had completely succumbed to the corporation. I was a wheel, turning round and round, doing the same thing day after day. I was another part of the machine.

There was no purpose or meaning in such a squalid existence. There was no point to my life if all I amounted to was being some manager at some discount retailer whose only aim was to make a profit. I was slowly killing myself for a job that didn't even matter, to make a bunch of money that I couldn't even enjoy because I had no time, no energy, and no strength. Nor could I bear to part with it. That way of life didn't make sense.

My refusal to listen to my body's signals and my heart's cries ultimately backfired. One cold day in December, with an impending night shift, I booked an early appointment at the chiropractor. I hadn't eaten much that morning, and I was cranky from the lack of calories by the time I returned from my appointment. I ended up overreacting about a benign comment that Raleigh had made, and in that moment, all the stresses and concerns and unwarranted anger I had been holding on to swelled up so suddenly, that the only way that I could think to release the emotions was to go for a run.

Given the fragility of my condition, I should have known better than to attempt a round on the treadmill when I barely had enough energy to maintain consciousness. But I didn't care. I wanted to be able to do something, anything, to distract myself from the mundane world. I wanted to escape the pressures that had been weighing down on me. Storming out of the desolate apartment, I walked briskly to the fitness center in the main office. I set the treadmill on high and ran until my lungs felt like they were going to burst.

The rigorous activity had the anticipated effect of releasing some of the negative energy I had bottled up inside, but it inadvertently pushed my delicate condition in an unexpected direction. As I undressed to take a shower, I examined my skeletal body, surprised to discover that it had not only swelled up, but featured splotches of pink and purple. In my famished state, I thought that perhaps I was imagining the swelling and color change, and got into the shower.

The water was actually hot for once, so I took advantage of the rarity by taking an especially long, leisurely shower. The swelling and the disturbing hues only worsened, but I attributed the phenomena to the heat of the water. Thick steam collected in the poorly ventilated space. I pushed through the dizziness that ensued, and stayed in the shower until the skin on my fingers puckered into soft raisins.

As I stepped out of the shower, I realized that I wasn't imagining the purple puffiness of my arms and legs. I pressed my finger against the swollen skin and watched it dimple. The indentation stayed white for several seconds before resuming its shade of pink-infused purple. I attributed my bloated body to an unexpected accumulation of fat, or at the very least the dilation of my blood vessels from all of the hot water, and continued to get ready for work. I ignored the warning signs that something was seriously wrong.

    With a long ten-hour shift still ahead of me, I forced myself to eat a bowl of soup despite the mild wave of nausea that had seized my stomach. The clock was ticking, and it was almost time to leave, so I fixed my wet hair into a quick bun and started to brush my teeth. As I stood there, examining my bloated, blotchy face in the bathroom mirror and lathering my teeth in white, foamy paste, an overwhelming sense of despair consumed me. My brushing slowed, until it stopped completely. Dizziness swooped in, and I suddenly felt the entire world pushing down on me. And suddenly, having barely spat out my toothpaste in time, I was on the bathroom floor.

Chapter 18

Raleigh heard me crying uncontrollably in the bathroom and came to my rescue. "What's wrong?" he asked, crouching over me and trying to hold me still. My whole body shook systematically as my legs kicked out in steady, repeated motions. My hands opened and closed, alternating from clenched fists to widespread palms. Air escaped my lungs. I couldn't get enough of it, and without enough oxygen, I couldn't feel my extremities.

I was numb. My eyes were glued shut and I was slipping out of consciousness. Raleigh, even with all of his concern, sounded so far away. He felt so distant. I could see myself lying there on the bathroom floor, with him hunched over my frail frame, as if from above. "I can't. I can't," I heard myself say.

"You can't what?" Raleigh asked frantically.

My words came out in bursts as I continued—and failed—to catch my breath. "I can't—feel anything," I cried. "I can't! I can't!" Tears drenched my face. My whole body writhed.

Raleigh lifted me off the bathroom floor and carried me to the bedroom. He set me on the bed and pulled the sheet over my body. In an effort to calm me, he put on a CD of handpicked selections of calming classical music. He left the room in hopes that the peaceful music and the solitude would console me.

Unfortunately, I didn't calm down. I worked myself up into

such a heightened state of hysteria that Raleigh took me to the hospital. He did so for my own good, not knowing that in my darkest moment, all I wanted was to die. As he carried me down the stairs through the snow and frantically drove me to the hospital, I was angry with him for saving me, especially at such a high financial cost. But ultimately, his refusal to accept the silent decision I had made was worth it.

The Universe had other plans for me. It wouldn't let me take the easy way out, escape all my troubles by ending my existence. While I didn't actually leave this earth, I did die that day, or at least a part of me did. I wasn't physically sick, but I was mentally ill. I was so fed up with work, with that crappy apartment, and with trying so hard to feel better, that I had lost hope. I had given up. That part of me, the part that so desperately clung to control despite all of the warning signs that I wasn't strong enough to carry the weight of the world on my shoulders, died in that hospital bed when I realized that all my efforts were futile. The Universe was in control. I needed to stop taking matters into my own hands and trust the Universe.

All that time that I had been trying to take control of my own life, trying to find affordable housing, a well-paying job, and an inexpensive health care plan, the Universe had another path laid out for me. Even though I had blatantly ignored the signs, the Universe had been guiding me all along, watching over me as I continued to plow my own path. After all, I had won the discount for the massage voucher despite the odds. There was an opening for an assistant manager in the very city to which I wanted to relocate. And the Universe had kept me safe as I learned my way around the unfamiliar streets and daunting neighborhoods. It was there the whole time, patiently waiting for me to realize the error of my ways and seek divine guidance.

STRESS SIZE

That's what the doctor who had spoken with me about taking anxiety medication didn't seem to understand. I was sick of trying to figure out what was wrong with me, sick of trying to do it all by myself. Medicine would only mask the symptoms. It wouldn't solve the problem. If I was stressed out and anxious, it was because I was trying too hard to cling to control. I needed to let go of all that worry. I needed to learn how to trust, how to live by faith. No amount of medicine, or even chiropractic adjustments or massage therapy, could do that for me. It was something I needed to do on my own.

As I stared at the greasy mound of chicken, mashed potatoes, and corn that Raleigh had brought me, I took the meal as I sign that I could start trusting the Universe by relinquishing my stringent control of my calorie consumption. It was a small gesture when there were so many much larger issues that needed to be addressed, but as I lay in the bed hooked up to the IV, it was the best that I could do. I cut into the chicken and smothered it in a dollop of creamy mashed potatoes. The saltiness soothed me. The hearty meal was so deliciously fattening, so nourishing, that I knew it was meant for me even though the slip on the tray said "Patient Name: Carol" and listed a different room number. The greasy food was a gift from heaven, a miraculous mistake made by the attendant who had handed the platter to Raleigh.

As I dug into the decadent brownie that was even larger than the serving of chicken, I wondered how much smoother the past year would have transpired if I had only been patient and waited for the Universe to guide me. I had been so anxious for immediate answers that I jumped into a series of rash decisions that ultimately brought me to that hospital bed. I couldn't keep doing that, keep relying on my own strength and fallible wisdom—not if I had any hope of recovering from my condition. As I wiped up the last few chocolate crumbs with my finger I knew, deep in my gut, what I needed to do.

    I needed to quit my job.

Chapter 19

EVEN THOUGH I KNEW I NEEDED TO QUIT MY JOB, NOT JUST for the sake of my health but as an offering to the Universe that I was relinquishing control of my life, I still struggled to part with the money. After all, Raleigh was only working part-time as a private tutor. We needed to be able to pay the bills, and I was the only one working full-time. I knew what I needed to do, and yet, I didn't do it.

Meanwhile, the Universe was speaking to me through the pastor at the church we started visiting. The original church I had looked up on the internet during our first week in the city didn't work out, so we headed over to our second choice. With my hectic work schedule, we couldn't make it to the sermon every Sunday, but we went whenever we were able. From the very first service that we attended, the topics were almost frighteningly relevant and applicable to my life. Every sermon pertained to listening to our bodies, taking care of our health out of respect for the temple that the Universe had given us, staying true to our passions by utilizing our spiritual gifts, and so on. The pastor's words pierced my heart. But even still, I didn't listen.

When I ignored the calling, the Universe sent me another sign in the form of yet another unexpected wave of illness. The day started off much like all the other days before. With the extended holiday hours, I was scheduled to come into work at a much later time. Sometimes I was scheduled to arrive as late as two or three o'clock in the afternoon so I could close up the store in the dead of the night. Not exactly an ideal situation for someone with dwindling stamina, but the shifted schedule opened up my mornings for other activities, usually paying bills, doing laundry, or balancing the checkbook. Sleeping in would have been senseless—it would have thrown off my sleep cycle for the days I would actually have to be at work early.

One particular day, not long after my visit to the hospital, I woke up early, went to the chiropractor, went for a slow walk on the treadmill, and took yet another nice, hot shower. By the time I finished drying off, got dressed, and started preparing my meal to take to work, I began experiencing the same wave of sickness that had seized me before—an immense heaviness and overwhelming fatigue, as if all I needed to do was sleep for years and years and I would be cured.

"It's all in my head," I thought to myself, tossing the salad I would be eating for dinner later. Wasn't that what the doctor had said, that it was an anxiety attack? If that was the case, then I could talk myself out of it.

I tried to ignore the symptoms and remain calm, but within minutes the fatigue was accompanied by a heavy pressure and sharp pain in my chest that radiated to my arms and legs. A sick feeling swam in the pit of my stomach. Weakness consumed me. I could barely hold the knife in my hand, let alone chop the vegetables before me. I braced my body against the counter, closed my eyes, and tried to breathe deeply to stabilize myself.

"Are you okay, honey?" Raleigh asked upon discovering me in the kitchen.

"I don't feel well," I whispered.

"What's wrong? Is there something I can help you with?"

"No, no, I'll be fine." I replied, attempting to resume my preparations. I still had to finish chopping my carrots and cucumbers, gather the accompanying dip, get some granola for my yogurt, refill my water bottle, and ensure that I had enough herbal tea to get me through the evening. Meanwhile, the neon green of the microwave clock warned me that I was beginning to run out of time. I would barely have enough time to finish packing my dinner and eat my lunch.

"Are you sure?" Raleigh asked, dubious. "Here, let me help you with that." He reached for the knife in an attempt to take over my task.

"No, I'm fine," I insisted. It took every ounce of strength I had left in me to slice the carrots. Slow, slow slices. Painful. And then there was the cucumber. Even slower, as my strength was draining.

Raleigh watched me for a moment, arms crossed and countenance concerned. He saw straight through my lies. "Maybe you should call out from work," he suggested as I fumbled to secure my painstakingly sliced vegetables in a plastic baggie.

"I can't call out from work," I said sadly. "I'm the closing store manager. Besides, I called out the other day. I can't do that again. They'll fire me." Calling out once was bad enough, calling out twice was unforgiveable, no matter how poorly I felt.

"They won't fire you," my husband said. "You're *sick*. They'll understand."

"I'm fine!" I insisted.

He continued to watch me, not fully believing that my words matched my condition, but when I successfully completed zipping the bag shut, he left the kitchen. I slowly finished getting ready. Since Raleigh had a tutoring appointment that evening, he took me to work. During the entire drive, he kept looking over at me in the passenger seat, growing paler by the second. He kept asking if I was okay, and I kept insisting that I was, even though I really wasn't.

By the time we arrived at the store, I was so weak that I could barely stand on my own. The slightest movement made me feel like I was going to plummet to the floor. Raleigh had to walk me across the parking lot as I clung to him for support. I couldn't possibly manage a two-story retail store in such a state, especially not with the extended holiday hours and last-minute shopping rush.

The associates eyed me curiously as I walked in, clutching onto Raleigh to keep from falling to the ground. "Hey, how's it going?" they asked slowly, eyebrows furrowed with concern. "You don't look so good."

"I don't feel so good," I whispered through cold, pale lips.

"What's wrong?" they asked. But I couldn't find the strength to answer.

"Will you be okay?" Raleigh asked, examining my pallor. He had successfully dragged me into the store, and it was time for me to start my shift. "I can take you home," he suggested. "I still have time before my lesson."

"But I'm already here," I replied. It didn't make sense for me to leave, not when I had already made it all the way out there. He squinted his eyes, as if to contest my decision, but he kissed me goodbye and wished me luck. I crawled up the stairs slowly, step by step, holding on to the side rail the entire time to keep from tumbling back down.

Donna shot me a dubious look as I entered the office. "You look terrible," she said. Not easily distracted, she quickly resumed her task on the computer.

"I feel awful," I replied, setting my purse and my lunch down on my desk.

She didn't even look away from her screen as she asked, "What's wrong?"

"It's that same sort of feeling I had that night I called out. Like I might pass out."

"Sit down for a while," she suggested. "Then when you're feeling better, you can get back to work," she said as she continued to click the mouse.

"A while" turned into two hours. With an overwhelming sense of nausea consuming me, all I wanted to do was hold the trashcan tightly against my chest. I stayed in my huddled position until Donna grew tired of me sitting in the chair while on the clock. She kept asking me if I was okay, all while hinting that I needed to get some work done. She pressured me into being productive.

"In my mind, I know I'm fine, but my body feels sick," I explained. "My mind is there, but my body isn't," I told her as I continued to clutch the trash can to my chest. The leftover french fries someone had tossed in the can certainly didn't help my nausea. As much as I didn't want to throw up in front of her, I almost wished that I would, to be rid of the sickening sensation.

"Well, then, if your mind's okay, maybe you can get some work done," she said, entirely unfazed by my fetal position. She rolled me in front of the computer screen with a complicated spreadsheet of the following week's schedule. The schedule featured a disarray of names, dates, times, and tasks. The information on the screen was as jumbled as my stomach. Even if I had been feeling well, I wouldn't have known what to do with all of that confusing information. Donna asking me to dive into the middle of that mess was a recipe for disaster. But at least working on the schedule didn't require me to stand up or walk around.

Donna left the office to check on the sales floor and the cashiers. I was all alone in the office, stewing in my illness and confusion.

Meanwhile, Ted, who had been the previous manager on shift, was leaving for the day. He stepped into the office to grab his coat, only to find me staring blankly at the screen. I hadn't budged an inch since Donna had left me there.

"Are you going to be okay?" he asked, sticking his face in front of mine.

I avoided his gaze, embarrassed about my condition. "No," I replied, tears rolling down my face.

"Take it easy," he said, holding his leather coat in his hands. "Don't stress yourself out. You're going to be okay."

I knew that I was going to be okay, but only if I left the store. I couldn't stay there to finish my shift, not if I had any chance of avoiding another episode of uncontrollable spasms. Ted left for the night, and I was alone again. I tried to blink through the nausea, breathe through the pain, but nothing worked.

"I'm not going to make it," I said weakly when Donna later walked back into the office.

Terror seized her eyes. I could see the wheels in her mind turning as she contemplated having to stay until midnight. Working that late would have rounded off a thirteen-hour shift for her. "Are you sure?" she asked, panicked.

I grabbed the trash can again and fought back another wave of nausea. "I'm sure," I replied sadly.

"Well, I can't stay," she asserted. "I've been here since eleven. You'll have to call the other area supervisor to see if she can cover for you."

"But it's her day off," I contested. I treasured my time off. If someone else had been sick and called out of work, I would have had a hard time mustering up the courage and strength to come in. And besides, from what I had heard after my last visit to the hospital, that area supervisor had worked a split shift to fulfill my responsibilities as the closing manager. I couldn't very well ask her to do the same favor again, not even two weeks later.

"She'll understand," Donna asserted.

If it were me, I wouldn't have understood. "She's going to hate me," I said softly.

"She'll get over it."

I looked at the reference sheet posted by the telephone and dialed the supervisor's number. The phone rang and rang, so I left a message.

"Hi... it's Nicole," I wavered. "I'm really sick. I'm not... I'm not going to make it. I'm really sorry. Is there any way you can cover for me? I'm so sorry. I'm sorry," I sobbed.

Donna and I both crossed our fingers that she would get the message and come in to cover my closing shift. With the spasms starting up, I asked Donna to look up the directions to the nearest hospital in case my condition worsened and I needed to seek medical attention. I struggled to maintain my grasp of the phone as I called Raleigh to come pick me up. He canceled his lesson and in the midst of rush-hour traffic, turned around to head in my direction.

With Raleigh stuck in traffic, I was at least a half hour away from being able to go home. Meanwhile, the spasms worsened. My legs kicked out from underneath me in rhythmic patterns. My hands opened and closed repeatedly. I had felt all of this before. I knew what to expect. I kept calm and concentrated on breathing. I took big, deep breaths as I prayed. This time, I prayed not for death as I had before, but for life. I prayed for there to be meaning in all of the pain, for there to be purpose behind my horrible experiences. "Keep me safe," I whispered. "Keep me calm."

Focused on breathing and prayer, my mind remained calm as my body continued to spasm uncontrollably. As the only other functioning manager in the store, Donna had left the office to tend to the store's operations. Meanwhile, I was alone in the office, struggling to maintain consciousness. I mustered the strength to crawl out of the office to sit outside the door so that Raleigh would see me when he finally arrived.

When Raleigh came, I realized that I had locked all my belonging inside of the office, including my keys to the door. He ran back downstairs to borrow a key from Donna. He seemed to be gone forever. I wasn't sure I could hold on. I kept praying for strength, for the Universe to guide me and see me through the terrifying experience.

"What took you so long?" I whispered when he returned, struggling to catch my breath. I thought I was going to die.

"It's so busy down there," Raleigh gasped, also out of breath from the short burst of activity. "The line is going past the ropes! She's swamped."

I felt bad, but there wasn't anything I could do. The situation was beyond my control. Raleigh unlocked the office door and grabbed my stuff from the desk. With my purse and my lunch bag looped around one arm, he supported me with the other. I leaned the entire weight of my body onto Raleigh as he practically carried me out of the store.

"Where am I going?" he asked. "Am I taking you home? Do you need to go to the hospital?"

I muttered something about a piece of paper in my purse. The directions that Donna had written down for me came in handy as Raleigh navigated through yet another unfamiliar part of town to take me to the doctor. Whatever was wrong with me wasn't a panic attack. It was something far more serious.

In the car, I thought I was going to die. My arms and legs swung out wildly. I couldn't control my own body. I kept my

STRESS SIZE

eyes closed to fight the nausea, but I could tell from the way the car swerved that Raleigh was winding down a twisting road and possibly getting lost. Finally, we pulled up to the hospital. There wasn't a complimentary valet service like there had been at the other hospital, so he left the car illegally parked in front of the emergency room entrance as he shuffled me inside.

Since I was barely able to stand, an attendant brought over a wheelchair for me. My legs kicked against the footrest. I couldn't contain my arms or legs. I couldn't breathe. I heard a triage nurse say there was an hour wait to be admitted. Raleigh raised his voice, desperate for me to receive medical attention. But there wasn't anything that could be done. There simply weren't enough beds.

He wheeled me into the waiting room. The wheelchair rattled as my spasms worsened. I felt like my lung was collapsing as I gasped for breath. I heard the people next to me complain about the unfairness of it all. "What's the matter with these people?" they said, even while dealing with their own medical issues. I started to suffocate; an hour wait would have inevitably killed me. "Can't they see she needs help?" they cried as they observed my worsening condition.

I wasn't going to make it. There wasn't enough oxygen getting into my lungs to sustain me. "I can't...breathe..." I muttered, struggling to find words. Meanwhile, in my head, I never stopped praying.

"What?" Raleigh asked.

"I can't...breathe..." I said again, slowly, painfully. *Please help me*, I continued to think.

Raleigh lost it. He ran back to the triage nurse and started yelling. "She can't breathe! She can't breathe!" Suddenly, a flurry of attendants was by my side. Somebody slipped an oxygen mask over my face and wheeled me through a set of doors into a corridor. In a small room with a bed, a nurse stood by holding a plastic bag. She asked me what was wrong, but I couldn't answer. Instead, I threw up into the bag that she held out in front of me just in time to catch the spillage. The nurse grimaced, but tied the bag up and tossed it into a biohazard receptacle.

The nurse helped me into the bed, but I was kicking so hard that the sheets wouldn't stay on me. I shivered, not only from the spasms, but from the chilly air-conditioned hospital. The nurse hooked me up to an IV and attempted to give me a dose of the same anxiety medication that the doctor at the other hospital had prescribed but I had refused to get filled. I tried to deny the medication, but Raleigh shot me a stern look and nodded at the nurse to proceed with slipping the medicine into the IV. There wasn't any arguing with him, not when I didn't have the strength to even speak. The nurse drew some blood then left the room with my samples. With the medicine streaming into my body, my muscles relaxed, and a new sense of serenity washed over me.

Every once in a while, my muscles still twitched, the jerking of which triggered a beep from one of the machines hooked up to me, but at least my spasms were under control. Raleigh stayed by my side, holding my hand. He didn't say a word, only watched me with love and concern. I concentrated on breathing and the belief that everything was going to be okay.

Different staff members shuffled past the open door of the room. Nobody seemed to be concerned about me or the frightening situation that had occurred. I was scared, since it was the second time in two weeks that this had happened to me. I was hoping to finally get some answers. Finally, after the hundredth oblivious employee passed by, a nurse came in and asked me if I needed anything.

"I'm so thirsty," I croaked. My throat was parched and my voice emerged in scratchy whispers.

"I'm sorry, honey," she replied. "The doctors said not to let you drink anything until they run some more tests."

"What tests?" I asked, but she had already started walking away.

A doctor came in and introduced himself. He asked if I had ever experienced anything like that episode before. I told him about my previous visit to the hospital, how the other doctor thought that it was an anxiety attack but I wasn't so sure. This time around, I wasn't even thinking about anything stressful when the illness set in. And mentally, I had remained calm during the entire episode. I was convinced that the problem was physiological, not psychological.

He asked if there were any common factors, parts of my routine that were the same for each of the days I had experienced the frightening symptoms. I thought for a moment, reflecting upon the day's activities, and there were a few trends emerging. For starters, I had worked a late shift and gotten up early to go to my morning appointment at the chiropractor's office. After that, I had exercised. In the case of the first episode, I had gone for a fast run. But in the present case, I had only walked. Then, of course, there was always the possibility that I hadn't eaten enough, since I was still struggling with incessant nausea.

The doctor thought that perhaps I was having a stroke at the hands of the chiropractor, since that appeared to be the only other common factor apart from having ventured onto the treadmill. He left the room, and yet another nurse came in to take me to get an MRI. Even in my pain and suffering, I thought to have Raleigh re-park the car while I was getting the procedure done. There I was, with a hospital gown draped over my work clothes, and I was still barking orders and clinging to control.

In the MRI room, the nurse had me take off all my jewelry. I was nervous about leaving my wedding rings with a complete stranger, but I didn't have a choice. The procedure needed to be done, to eliminate the possibility that I had experienced a stroke. The nurse handed me an eye mask and a pair of earplugs, warning me that the machine would get very loud. It did, but that didn't stop me from falling asleep during the procedure.

When the MRI was done, the nurse wheeled me back to my room. Raleigh said I had been gone for an hour, but to me it felt like only minutes. I was cold, tired, hungry, and thirsty, but I was told I would have to wait for the results of the blood work and the MRI before I could be released. Raleigh and I waited in the room for several hours, growing bored with the basic cable programming on the television, before the doctor returned.

He told me that the only thing they could find was a severe case of hyponatremia. I hadn't ever heard of that before, and I told him as much. He explained that it was a low amount of sodium in the blood, which can cause muscle spasms.

"Do you eat a lot of salt?" he asked.

"Not really," I admitted. "I eat mostly fruits and vegetables. I don't add any salt to my food."

"Well, that's very healthy of you to be a vegetarian, but you should try eating something salty every once in a while."

"Like what?" I asked. I had always been under the impression that eating too much salt was a bad thing, so I had all but cut it out of my diet.

"Eat a cheeseburger and some french fries," he replied. That, in all his wisdom as a medical professional, was his official advice. So when the doctor finally released me from the hospital, Raleigh took me to a burger joint on the way home. I let go of control, and ate a big, greasy cheeseburger and some french fries.

Chapter 20

AFTER THAT SECOND HOSPITAL VISIT, I KNEW THAT THE Universe was trying to get through my hard head. My stubbornness had nearly killed me, but I still had the notion that I needed to keep working to survive. Since I still hadn't really learned my lesson, I kept getting sick. I knew it was the Universe's way of telling me that I needed to slow down, but I kept chugging along anyway.

In addition to experiencing two peculiar episodes of uncontrollable spasms, a joint in one of my toes swelled up to twice its normal size. The pain and inflammation were so severe that by the second week of leaving it untreated, I could barely walk. But I was sick of doctors, sick of not finding any answers, and I refused to seek medical attention for my ailment. I continued to hobble through the store, denying that I had a problem. It was only when I received a phone call from my gynecologist, reminding me it was time for my free annual checkup, that I took it as a sign from the Universe that I needed to pull myself together.

The doctor, after sending me all over town to get my pathetic toe x-rayed, determined that I had an infection in the bone. She prescribed an antibiotic. Since I already had enough intestinal issues as it was, I was paranoid about losing the bacteria in my stomach, so I self-prescribed a probiotic to counteract the loss of fauna. My infection went away, but the overgrowth of yeast in my system resulted in a painful rash that covered most of my fingers. But I let that condition slide too, until I couldn't even use my fingers anymore. I had to see a dermatologist to make headway. I still hadn't heeded the warnings that I was on the wrong path, and my ailments never seemed to cease.

Meanwhile, my periods had become irregular again. The gynecologist, who still couldn't find anything wrong with me, referred me to an endocrinologist. The specialist ran all sorts of tests, and even analyzed my nutritional intake, and apart from a mild Vitamin D deficiency, still couldn't find a cause for my symptoms. Since I was working at a stressful job with an irregular schedule, she suggested that I try seeing a sleep specialist.

That was the last straw. I had lost my patience with doctors. It was clear that there was a connection between my stress level and my sickness. The more that I turned away from divine wisdom and tried to seek out answers on my own, the more my symptoms worsened. I couldn't keep fighting for control. I couldn't keep working at that job. It was slowly killing me.

I spoke with Donna at work and insisted on taking a demotion. She was sad to see me go, but only because it was inconvenient for her to be short an assistant manager. At any rate, she facilitated my transfer to another location that was still fairly close to my apartment, and I started working there part-time as an associate.

Even with the reduced hours and minimized stress, I still felt like I was forcing myself to do something that I wasn't supposed to be doing. It didn't feel right, and I was still sick. The Universe was calling me in a different direction, to utilize my creative talents. Since I had studied art in college, I started searching for an art-related career. That seemed like as good as a direction as any, and certainly better than the way I had been heading.

Within a couple of weeks, I landed several interviews. Coordinating transportation was difficult, especially with Raleigh having found a position as a long-term substitute at a local high school. I scheduled my interviews whenever I had a couple of hours free, which often meant taking Raleigh to work, driving across town, and picking him back up later in the day.

For one particular interview, the only time I could squeeze it in was on a Saturday morning. That was better for me anyway, since Raleigh had the day off and I could use the car at my leisure. But I should have paid more attention to the weather forecast, because it snowed that morning. I peeled back the blinds to peek at the snow blowing sideways. "Maybe I should call to reschedule," I wondered.

"That's up to you," Raleigh responded from his usual spot on the couch. "It's *your* job interview."

"But won't it look bad if I call to reschedule?"

"Honey, it's a *blizzard*. I'm sure they'll understand."

"Yeah, but will *I* understand?" That would be my third interview in a matter of days. The position was for an assistant art conservator, the ideal career for someone with my creative background. The job was art-related and I thought I would enjoy it. Besides, my symptoms were starting to flare up again, even with the part-time position at a different store. I needed to find a new job—and fast.

I wiped the fog from the inside of the window. Surely the snow couldn't be that bad. "I'll be okay," I concluded. I got dressed and braved the storm.

"Be careful," Raleigh said as I walked out the door. "And good luck!"

My trusty GPS guided me through an unfamiliar part of town. But even if I had ventured out that way before, I wouldn't have recognized the streets. A thick blanket of snow disguised the entire scene.

In my effort to beat the weather and arrive on time, I pulled up to the shop nearly twenty minutes early. I shivered in the car as I awaited my appointment time. It didn't take long for my windshield to become encrusted with stark white snow.

The interview itself started out smoothly. The woman asked about my experience and qualifications and I answered with confidence and charm. The situation was looking fairly promising. That was, until I learned that the company was looking for someone to work full-time, possibly with overtime hours. The interviewer asked if this would be a problem.

"Unfortunately, I'm only available to work part-time," I replied. "My husband and I share the car, and I have to take him to work and pick him up each day."

"What about public transportation?" the woman suggested. "Couldn't one of you take the bus or the light rail?"

"We live very far from here, and from his job," I explained. "The light rail doesn't go out that way, and it would be an hour bus ride for him. I couldn't ask him to do that, not with this weather."

"Well, I see," the interviewer frowned. She asked a few more brief questions, thanked me for my time, and sent me on my way.

As I headed back home on the highway, I was disappointed that my transportation situation and limited availability had ruined my chances of obtaining a new position. However, I didn't hesitate to thank the Universe for the opportunity anyway. No sooner had I finished my silent prayer, than my steering wheel starting turning on its own.

My car began sliding sideways.

I knew there was nothing I could do to prevent the inevitable. I let go of the wheel and made my peace with the impending crash as my car careened toward the SUV in the next lane.

But I didn't crash. The SUV changed lanes moments from impact. One disaster averted, but my car now spun toward the concrete divider.

"Please protect me," I prayed.

I watched as my front bumper missed the median by an inch.

Realistically, I should have crashed. I should have hit the car next to me, and when I didn't, I should have hit the concrete. But the Universe was in control, guiding my car as it slid along the black ice.

After completing three and a half spins, I finally slowed to a stop. Five lanes of halted freeway traffic faced me. Not a single car budged. The other drivers waited patiently as I regained control, turned my car around, and proceeded, albeit slowly. I thought I had control, but clearly, I didn't. The Universe was in control the whole time.

Chapter 21

As I waited to hear back from the interviewers, Raleigh and I continued to go to church. Attending the weekly services was much easier now that I was only working part-time. I had negotiated with my new manager to have Sundays off in exchange for being willing to work on Saturdays. I was grateful, too, because the sermons at church became even more relevant. The Universe was speaking to me through the services.

One Sunday, there was a guest couple that shared their testimony. The husband described how he had uprooted his family in order accept a well-paying job in another state. They hadn't sold their current house, and went on to purchase another in their new location. As the job didn't work out and they fell further and further into debt, they realized that they had made a terrible mistake. They had been taking matters into their own hands instead of trusting the Universe, which resulted in the disaster of bankruptcy. With the exception of going broke, their story sounded just like mine.

The pastor also shared a story about a friend of his who had a lucrative career with excellent benefits. The friend had finally achieved his dream of wealth and power, but the position was meaningless. He would get to work before the sun had risen, and leave after it had already set. As he slipped into a deep depression, he realized that his mundane responsibilities were slowly stripping him of his humanity. He abandoned his career without so much as a job prospect, with only the unwavering belief that the Universe would provide.

That story gave me the courage to finally put an end to the path that I had been crawling along. No amount of money or achievement was worth sacrificing my health. Nothing was worth sacrificing my connection to the Divine. Without so much as another job offer, the next day I put in my two weeks' notice for my part-time position. I was finally learning to trust in the Universe.

That same day, I received a phone call from one of the companies I had interviewed with. It was for the art restoration position, the job I had interviewed for before nearly spinning out on the freeway. I'd thought for sure that I wouldn't get the position because they were looking for someone to work full-time, and I could only work part-time. The woman on the phone said that she was so impressed by my communication and honesty during the interview that she was willing to work around my schedule. She invited me in for a second interview to ensure that I would enjoy the type of work performed at the facility. The timing was too perfect to be a coincidence, so I went in for the second interview.

I ended up getting the job. I was thrilled, but also concerned. Given the fragility of my condition, I wasn't sure I would be able to handle all the chemicals that I would have to use to clean and repair works of art. The last thing I wanted was to have another relapse and end up in the hospital again. But I needed the money, and the timing seemed ideal, so I took the job despite my reservations.

I did okay at first. There was a heck of a learning curve for all of the procedures, but I got used to it. It helped that I was a quick learner. My supervisor was impressed with my work, which made the career change even easier. I found that I liked the job so much that when the semester ended and Raleigh was out of work, I transitioned to full-time.

Unfortunately for my stress level, the art conservation facility was on the other side of town. The commute was time-consuming, and I felt myself being stretched thin as I struggled to find enough time to work, drive, and run errands. I wasn't any better off than I had been while working in retail. I had switched positions, but nothing had really changed.

I thought maybe moving closer to my new job would help minimize my stress by freeing up more time. Our lease was ending at our decrepit apartment, and we couldn't really see ourselves committing to another full year. I looked into the apartments near my new job and was disappointed to discover that they cost at least one or two hundred dollars more than what we were currently paying. With the tight rental market, it was cheaper to buy than it was to rent. From having worked overtime every week for nearly eight months as an assistant manager, I had saved up quite a bit of money. Raleigh and I decided to take the plunge and buy a house.

In an ideal world, I would have liked to have saved up at least enough money to cover 20 percent of the purchase price and do a fifteen-year loan, but we only had enough for the minimum down payment for a thirty-year loan. With the end of our lease quickly approaching and the forty-five-minute commute becoming more and more tedious, I abandoned my original plan. Finding a suitable home with a short commute was more important than maintaining my particularities.

With the help of a patient realtor, Raleigh and I found a beautifully remodeled condo tucked away in the foothills. We instantly fell in love with the laminate floors, open floor plan, and spacious bathroom. Everything in the unit was so new and so clean. The only thing it needed was a fresh coat of paint. We immediately envisioned ourselves living there in the cozy condo. Since the unit was located less than five miles away from my new job, my commute would be cut to a mere ten minutes. We were sold.

No sooner did we enter escrow than I started feeling sick again. Not a day passed that I didn't experience nausea or some sort of ache or pain. Unfortunately, since I wasn't working as an assistant manager anymore, I no longer had the health insurance that had previously enabled me to seek medical care. To make matters worse, the comparatively modest wages that I earned at my new job still put me just past the cutoff for being eligible for state health insurance. I couldn't catch a break.

After reading the denial letter from the state health insurance office, I enrolled in a partially state-funded discount program that would limit the amount I would have to pay for certain services. Unfortunately, the coverage could only be used at certain facilities, none of which were near either my current apartment or my anticipated dwelling. But I figured that a discount was better than nothing, especially if my mild illness worsened into more severe symptoms as it had in the past.

However limited, the discounted services came in handy when, after doing too much heavy lifting in the overly warm restoration facility, I nearly fainted. With the nausea in my gut and the pain and pressure in my chest, I could feel another attack coming on. I had experienced those same unpleasant sensations before, prior to my unexpected hospital visits, so I knew better than to ignore my symptoms. I explained my situation to my supervisor and informed her that I would need to leave early.

Raleigh, who was at a private tutoring appointment when I

called him, came and picked me up from work as soon as he was finished. He took me to the nearest hospital that would accept my discount program. Even then, the facility was nearly half an hour away. By the time we arrived, all that remained of my disturbing symptoms were some mild chest pain and an overwhelming sense of fatigue. The triage nurses eyed me skeptically as I braced myself against the counter and slowly explained my situation. In their eyes, I seemed fine. After all, I was still walking and talking. I needed to be dead or dying to be seen immediately.

We sat for several hours in the cramped waiting room before a nurse came in and called my name. I was relieved to finally be admitted to the emergency room. I was hoping to find some answers to my health concerns. But again, after checking all my vitals and drawing blood, the doctors didn't know what was wrong with me. They didn't have the time or patience to dig deeper into my dilemma, and so they sent me on my way.

As I sat in the passenger seat of the car, utterly disappointed as Raleigh drove us home, I knew I had made yet another mistake. I had rushed into another job when I hadn't given my body enough time to properly heal. I had thought that because the timing was perfect, it was a sign from the Universe that the new job was the right choice, but I could see how I was still clinging to control. I was trying to rely on my own strength, and that wasn't enough. Only the Universe could guide me through my difficult times.

I knew that the Universe was calling me to follow a different path, but I couldn't very well quit while Raleigh and I were in the middle of buying the house we so desperately craved. I grimaced through the pain and continued working, keeping the finish line in mind. Each day I prayed to for enough energy and strength to see me through my shift. Making it through each day was

STRESS SIZE

hard enough, but I needed to close on the condo before I even contemplated quitting my job.

The closer we drew to the closing date, the more my symptoms worsened. In addition to the muscle weakness and incessant nausea, I started seeing spots, dark shadows, bright flashing lights, and changes in colors. I had a hard time focusing on small details, and I started making mistakes on priceless works of art. I knew that I couldn't continue working in that detail-oriented position, not when my health and the integrity of artwork was at stake.

I visited an eye doctor, who conducted nearly a dozen different tests to evaluate the health of my eyes. After being examined for nearly two hours, he determined that the actual health of my eye was fine and that in fact, my prescription had improved. I couldn't understand how that could be the case when I was experiencing such frightening symptoms. He explained that whatever changes I was experiencing in my vision were neurological. There was something wrong with my brain.

I couldn't afford to see a neurologist. Even if I could have afforded one, I wouldn't have been able to see one. I had been on a waiting list for an appointment to see a regular physician since I had enrolled in the discounted medical program several months before. Even if I could have obtained a referral, it would likely have been several more months before I could see a specialist. Meanwhile, I couldn't continue to butcher irreplaceable works of art.

Clearly, the Universe still had other plans for me. I hadn't been patient, and I had jumped into a position that still wasn't quite right for me. It was using the startling changes in my vision to warn me that after all the pain and suffering I had endured, I was still trying to do everything by myself. That being the case,

I put in my notice at work. I quit my second job in a matter of months, but I didn't care. All that mattered was that I was finally letting go. I released my control and surrendered to the Divine.

Epilogue

AFTER QUITTING MY SECOND JOB, A PART OF ME FELT USELESS, like I had failed. For someone who had always been an A+ student, top performer, and general overachiever, quitting was the same thing as failing. But that wasn't the case. Resigning meant relinquishing control, putting my trust in the Universe, and realizing that the more I tried to do things on my own, the more devastating the results. Relying on my own strength was a proven recipe for disaster. I needed to put my faith in something solid.

So I quit my job, trusting that the Universe had a plan for me and everything would work out for the greater good. The day after I put in my notice, I received an email announcing a book publishing contest. The timing couldn't have been more perfect. Now that I was unemployed for the foreseeable future, I could finally tell the story that the Universe had been urging me to share. I could finally tell the world how my quest for control had nearly killed me. It was only by giving up control, and trusting the Universe completely, that I finally started to heal.

By the time I learned about the contest, the submission deadline was a little over a month away. I still had to finish my last two weeks of work, and I hadn't even written the first word of my story. Raleigh wondered if I would be able to finish my book in time. I told him that if it was meant to be, that the Universe would give me the words to write and the strength to write them. And it did. I finished my manuscript in one month.

Although I didn't win the contest, I was a finalist and being recognized gave me the confidence I needed to keep sharing my story. I became a mental health advocate and volunteered to help other people manage stress and navigate life's challenges. Connecting with people made me realize that I wasn't the only one who struggled with stress, anxiety, and disordered eating. By sharing my story, I was able to help other people heal as well.

Eventually I found another job as an office manager for a small online retailer and went back to work. However, I did so with clearer boundaries for myself. I learned how to listen to my body and prioritize my self-care. I ate more, worried less, and managed my stress effectively. My weight returned to a healthy level, I didn't have as many aches and pains, and I looked and felt better.

Later, I had the opportunity to work from home as a virtual assistant. Working from home allowed me even greater freedom to honor my body's needs and take good care of myself. I was able to eat, exercise, and rest whenever I needed to, without the added pressure of commuting or trying to get along with colleagues. Being location-independent also gave me more flexibility in relocating. This came in handy when a couple of years later, my husband and I decided to sell our condo and move across town.

The work-at-home life also allowed me to seamlessly shift into better roles. Over the next few years, I went from being a virtual assistant, to a social media marketer, to an online business manager. Now, I'm an intuitive guide and spiritual mentor empowering people to listen to their soul's calling so they can pursue their purpose in life and become the best version of themselves. I've gone from being anxious to aligned.

STRESS SIZE

Having learned more about myself and how the Universe works, I believe that everything that I experience is to guide others through the same. As painful as my past may be, I wouldn't be able to do this kind of work without having personally experienced these trials and errors. It's said that whatever doesn't kill you makes you stronger, and it's true.

As my work situation improved and my body healed over the years, I didn't need to visit the doctor anymore. Medical intervention wasn't necessary—listening to my body was the cure I needed. Although I chose to occasionally visit my massage therapist and chiropractor, it was to maintain my health rather than to become healthy. I didn't "need" these services the way I felt I'd needed them before because I was no longer in a state of emergency. I'm now in a healthy place where I don't need to visit the chiropractor anymore, and getting a massage is a treat instead of a necessity.

It's been a long journey and I'm still a work in progress, but thankfully, my craving for control shifted into a desire to nurture my mind, body, and soul. I've learned how to treat myself with kindness and compassion. I'm patient with myself and remember that progress is progress, no matter how slow I go. While I might not always be in control of every situation, I'm *always* divinely supported. If I experience a challenge, I remember that for every bad day, there are so many other good ones. Most importantly, I understand that my success isn't measured by my dress size, stress level, or bank account, but my generosity of spirit, capacity to love, and willingness to shine my light in the world.

May you reduce your stress size and grow your heart instead.

www.ingramcontent.com/pod-product-compliance
Lightning Source LLC
Chambersburg PA
CBHW021100080526
44587CB00010B/323